100
HOT & SPICY
SAUCES

SALLY GRIFFITHS

PHOTOGRAPHS BY
SIMON WHEELER

WEIDENFELD
& NICOLSON
LONDON

CONTENTS

THE STORECUPBOARD

There is nothing more off-putting than the prospect of wasting valuable time searching for incomprehensible ingredients from far-flung countries. Bearing this in mind I have stuck to recipes made with herbs, spices and other ingredients currently available in most supermarkets, although I have to admit that it gives me great pleasure to track down small shops specialising in ethnic ingredients. The following list will enable you to make more than half the recipes without venturing beyond the front door!

Pulses and Grains

Canned or dried black beans, red kidney beans, black eyed beans, haricot beans, lentils, rice, couscous

Chillies

Dried chillies, fresh red and green chillies, chilli powder, dried chilli flakes, cayenne, paprika

Fresh Herbs

Coriander, mint, basil, parsley, chives

Fruit and Vegetables

Tomatoes, red peppers, green peppers, yellow peppers, cucumber, celery, garlic, shallots, onions, spring onions, lemons, limes, oranges

General Ingredients

Brown sugar, white sugar, black treacle, honey, dried apricots, coconut milk, cornflour, dried marjoram, canned pineapple, canned tomatoes, gherkins, capers, white wine, sherry, redcurrant jelly, peanut butter

In the Fridge

Plain or Greek yoghurt, crème fraîche, eggs, butter
• Keep cartons of fresh beef, chicken and vegetable stock in the freezer

Nuts

Once the packet has been opened, store in an airtight container.
Cashew nuts, pine nuts, walnuts, peanuts, pistachio nuts

Oils

Store in a cool, dark place.
Sunflower oil, olive oil, sesame oil, groundnut oil, walnut oil

Pastes

Unopened paste will last indefinitely. Once open, cover and use as quickly as possible. Store in the fridge.

Thai red curry paste, Thai green curry paste, tomato paste, Indian curry paste

Sauces

Japanese soy sauce, Tabasco, West Indian hot pepper sauce

Spices

Allspice, caraway seeds, cardamom pods, cinnamon, cloves, ground coriander, coriander seeds, ground cumin, cumin seeds, curry powder, fennel seeds, garam masala, fresh root ginger, lemon grass, dry mustard, mace, black mustard seeds, black peppercorns, green peppercorns in brine, salt, nutmeg, poppy seeds, saffron, sesame seeds, turmeric

Vinegars

Balsamic vinegar, rice wine vinegar, malt vinegar, white wine vinegar

ALL ABOUT CHILLIES

Originally from South America, chillies have been used as a food ingredient for at least 8,000 years, and were introduced to the rest of the world by the Portuguese and Spaniards in the 16th and 17th centuries. There are hundreds of different varieties grown all over the world, each with its own individual flavour and heat level. Chillies are without question the most important ingredient in almost all hot and spicy recipes.

What is the difference between red and green chillies? Most chillies are green in their unripened state. As they ripen they become red, yellow, orange or brown. In general, the redder the chilli, the sweeter the taste.

How can you tell a hot chilli from a mild one? It really is a question of experimentation, although there are some guidelines. See pages 10-11 on fresh and dried chillies.

What is the best way to keep fresh chillies? Wash, dry, wrap them in paper towels (not plastic bags which create moisture and hasten the spoiling process) and store in the refrigerator. Kept in the open, chillies will quickly shrivel and lose their flavour.

What should you look out for when buying fresh chillies? Choose brightly coloured, firm, unblemished chillies with smooth, unbroken skins. A sharp, clean smell is indicative of good fresh chillies.

Are fresh chillies used with or without their seeds? It largely depends on how hot you want the sauce to be. However, it is the vein that holds the seeds which creates the heat, so when removing seeds, take care to cut out the vein as well.

Do chillies irritate the skin? Chillies contain capsaicin, an oil which can cause skin irritation. Wash the afflicted area immediately with soapy water, and always wear rubber gloves when handling large quantities of chillies.

Can you freeze fresh chillies? Wash and dry fresh, good quality chillies, then split them in half, deseed, chop and lay flat on a tray. Pop the tray in the freezer and when the pieces are frozen, bag them. Defrost chillies before use. Roasted chillies can be frozen whole – the skins will come off easily when they are defrosted.

Can you reduce the heat level of chillies? Eating a hot chilli can take your breath away! A glass of water will cool you down temporarily, but try beer or some kind of spirit for longer-lasting relief. Cooking chillies (roasting, frying or grilling) will reduce the heat level, as will sugar, dairy products such as yoghurt, milk or ice-cream, or bananas and coconut milk.

What is the advantage of dried chillies? They are always on hand when you need them. The process of drying chillies concentrates the sugars and flavours, making them more of a spice.

How long can you keep dried chillies? Store in a plastic bag in the deep-freeze for 1-2 years or keep in an airtight container in a cool, dry, dark place for 8 months to a year maximum.

How do you know which chilli to buy when a recipe simply indicates 'chillies'? In this book every recipe has a heat level indicated in brackets beside the heading, for example: Green Chutney Sauce (mild-medium). You can then refer to the sections on fresh and dried chillies for the heat of each chilli – i.e. New Mexico green (mild-medium). The trick is to become acquainted with your own preferred heat level and to experiment accordingly.

How do you know when to use dried or fresh chillies? Some recipes require fresh chillies, others use dried. Very often it is simply a matter of choice or availability. As a general guide, fresh chillies give a wonderful 'crunch' in salsas and other fresh sauces, whereas dried chillies, which have a very distinctive flavour, are used mostly in sauces, stews and purées.

How do you adjust the heat of your sauce? If a sauce is too hot tone it down with rice, potatoes, dairy products, coconut milk or a touch of sugar.

FRESH CHILLIES

Most of the fresh chillies listed below are available in good supermarkets, delicatessens and specialist food shops.

Anaheim *green – mild – available all year*

Commonly known as the long green chilli. About 15 cm (6 inches) in length, with a distinct vegetable flavour. Good in stews and sauces.

Anaheim *red – mild – available October/November*

Also known as the long red chilli. Very versatile and sweeter than its green counterpart. Use in sauces, soups and stews

Caribe *yellow/pale green – hot – available all year*

Short chilli with a fresh, light flavour and sharp refined heat.

Caribe *pink/orange – hot-very hot – available all year*

Riper and sweeter than the yellow Caribe.

Chilaca *dark brown – medium – available September/October*

Long chilli, often curved. Good in sauces or pickled.

Cubanelle *yellow – mild-medium – available September/October*

Long chilli with a strong waxy flavour. Perfect for salads or sauces.

Cubanelle *red – mild-medium – available November*

Riper and sweeter than the yellow cubanelle.

Dutch *green – medium – available all year*

Sometimes referred to as the Holland chilli.

Dutch *red – medium – available all year*

Riper and sweeter than the green Dutch chilli.

Fresno *red – medium-hot – available October/November*

Small chilli often mistaken for the red jalapeño or serrano chilli. Excellent in salsas, pickled, or roasted and blended into sauces.

Habañero *orange – very hot – available September/October*

The hottest chilli in the world. Lantern-shaped, it measures about 5 cm (2 inches) in length. Use in salsas, seafood marinades and chutneys.

Habañero *red – very hot – available October/November*

Riper and sweeter than the orange habañero.

Jalapeño *green – medium – available all year*

Probably the most commonly used chilli. Thick-fleshed, 5-7.5 cm (2-3 inches) long, with a green vegetable flavour. Use it to spike up salsas, dips, stews and sauces.

Jalapeño *red – medium – available most of the year*

Has a sweeter flavour than the green jalapeño.

New Mexico *green – mild-medium – available September/October*

It measures 15-23 cm (6-9 inches) and has a sweet, earthy flavour. Excellent in green chilli sauce, stews and salsas.

New Mexico *dark red – medium – available October/November*

Ripened form of New Mexico green. Fleshy and sweet, use it in red chilli sauce, barbecue sauces and chutneys.

Poblano *dark green with purple-black tinge – mild – available all year*

Measures 10-12.5 cm (4-5 inches) in length. Always cooked, never eaten raw, the poblano is excellent roasted.

Scotch Bonnet *yellow-green, orange and red – very hot – available all year*

Similar in appearance to the habañero, it has a distinct smoky flavour. Used in many Caribbean dishes.

Serrano *bright green – hot – available all year*

A clean, biting heat. Perfect for salads, pickled or in sauces.

Serrano *red – hot – available all year*

Riper and sweeter than the green serrano.

Thai *bright green, or red when ripe – hot – available all year*

Measures about 4 cm (1 1/2 inches) and used mostly in southeast Asian cooking. Red Thais can also be used for decoration in salads and noodle dishes. When Thai chillies are unavailable, you can use 3 serrano chillies for each Thai chilli.

DRIED CHILLIES

As they dry the flavour of chillies intensifies, resulting in a distinctive smell and taste. Select clean, unbroken chillies with bright colours and a good aroma. Most dried chillies need to be reconstituted before use by soaking in hot water for 20 minutes. Then chop, shred or purée with a little of the soaking liquid until a moderately thick consistency is formed or prepare according to recipe instructions.

Ancho *orange-red – mild*

The most commonly used chilli in Mexico. Sweet and fruity. Excellent for stuffing. Also available in powdered form. Remove stalk, deseed and soak; split before stuffing. There is no need to skin.

Bird's Eye *bright orange – very hot*

Small, East African chilli with a sharp black pepper taste. Good whole – rather like a bay leaf – in soups, stews, piri piri sauces and for flavouring vinegars and oils. Can be crushed in a pestle and mortar.

Cascabel *dark reddish-brown – medium*

Small round chilli also known as 'little rattle' because of the sound it makes when shaken. It has a mild, nutty, woody flavour and is good in stews, soups, sauces and salsas. Remove stalk, deseed and soak, then scoop out the flesh with a teaspoon and mash in with the other ingredients.

Chipotle *coffee brown – medium-hot*

A large, dried and smoked jalapeño chilli, with a sweet nutty flavour. It is widely used in Mexican cooking. Remove stalk, soak, deseed and purée with a little of the soaking liquid.

Choricero *dark reddish brown – mild*

Large, very mild Spanish chilli, suitable for stuffing. Use to flavour soups, seafood dishes, stews, sauces, rice and bean dishes. Remove stalk, deseed and soak, then purée with a little of the soaking liquid.

Guajillo *dark brown – mild-medium*

10-15 cm (4-6 inches) long and slightly curved, this mild, sweet chilli has a green tea flavour. Use in salsas and sauces. Remove stalk, deseed and soak, then purée with a little of the soaking liquid and sieve.

Guindilla *deep red – medium*

Spanish chilli with a sweet flavour. Adds zip to sauces, stews and soups. Can be toasted (see page 14). Remove stalk, deseed and soak, then purée with a little of the soaking liquid and sieve.

Habañero *yellow-orange – very hot*

Dried form of the fresh habañero and very, very hot! Great in condiments, fish stews, curries and salsas. Remove stalk, deseed and soak, then purée with a little of the soaking liquid. To flavour a dish during cooking, dried habañeros can be added whole, then removed once the desired heat is acquired.

New Mexico *olive dark green – mild-medium*

Skinned, dried and roasted version of the fresh New Mexico green chilli. Has a sweet, smoky taste tinged with flavours of celery and dried apple. Use in powdered form to season soups and stews. Remove stalk and soak, then shred or chop and throw into the cooking pot.

New Mexico Red *bright red – mild*

Measuring 12.5-28 cm (5-7 inches), with a clean heat and an earthy, fruity flavour. Wonderful in red sauces. Remove stalk and soak, then purée with a little of the soaking water and sieve.

Pasado *dull orange-red – medium*

This is a New Mexico red chilli which has been roasted, then skinned and dried. It has a toasted flavour tinged with apple, celery and citrus. Good in soups and stews. Remove stalk and soak.

Pasilla *very dark brown – medium*

Long, thin and wrinkled, the pasilla tastes of berries and liquorice. Good with seafood and sauces. Remove stalk, shake out seeds and soak, then purée in a little of the soaking water or chop.

Tepin *red – very hot*

Small spherical shape, with a searing heat. This chilli has a dry, dusty flavour tinged with sweetcorn and nuts. Remove stalk, then crush on to food (use like a bay leaf).

Powdered and Crushed Chillies

Caribe *medium heat* crushed New Mexico chilli. **Chimayo** *sweet warm flavour* finest ground Mexico chilli. **Molido** *sweet earthy flavour* ground New Mexico chilli. **Pimenton de la Vera** *hot* finely ground Spanish oak-smoked chillies.

SPICES

Store spices in an airtight container in a cool, dark place. Buy in small quantities for optimum freshness.

Allspice

Grown mostly in Jamaica, its name aptly describes the flavour: a combination of cinnamon, cloves, pepper and nutmeg. Brought to Europe by the Spaniards in the 16th century, allspice is now used in cooking all over the world. The unripe green berries (the size of small peas) are dried in the sun and are only ready for use when they turn brown. To grind allspice, use a pestle and mortar or coffee grinder. It is also available ready ground.

Black Peppercorns

Pepper is the king of spices and was once literally worth its weight in gold. It accounts for one-quarter of the world's spice trade, India being the foremost producer. Black peppercorns are unripe green peppercorns which are left to ferment for a few days before being sun-dried. Freshly ground black pepper is used in many of the recipes. It has a strong, pungent flavour.

Caraway

Was used as a spice in the Stone Age. The small, dried seeds are brown and have a distinct, aromatic and spicy flavour. Delicious with vegetables and rich meats, and in cakes and breads. Caraway is mainly used in seed form but is also available ground.

Cardamom

The third most expensive spice in the world and grown extensively in India, Mexico and Guatemala, Cardamom is an important ingredient in Indian cooking, especially in pilaus and curries. In the Middle East and North Africa it is used to flavour sweetmeats, pastries and strong black coffee.

Green cardamom pods are the most common and have a strong, lemony flavour which enhances the flavour of both savoury and sweet dishes. Pods retain their flavour better than ground cardamom.

Cayenne

A very pungent spice ground from small ripe chillies of the *Capsicum frutescens* variety. It has been used in Western cooking since the 18th century.

Cinnamon

Native of Sri Lanka and now grown in many other wet, tropical countries. One of the oldest spices, it is the bark of a small evergreen tree, peeled, rolled and then dried. It has a pleasant woody aroma and a warm, fragrant taste. In Europe cinnamon is used mainly in cakes, biscuits and sweet dishes, but in the Middle East it is used to flavour savoury dishes such as stews and curries.

Cloves

Take their name from the Latin *clavus*, meaning nail. Indeed these dried, unopened flower buds, native to the Spice Islands, do resemble nails. Grown in a tropical, maritime climate, cloves are aromatic but taste bitter on their own. Once cooked they give rich flavour, instantly recognisable in cakes, biscuits and mulled wine. Cloves are also used to flavour meat dishes, chutneys and marinades.

Coriander

Native to southern Europe and the Middle East, coriander is a member of the carrot family and is used in cooking all over the world. In India both leaves and seeds are used extensively in curries. The Moroccan seeds more commonly available here have a milder taste than the Indian variety and a spicy aroma.

Cumin

Grown in many warm countries and used extensively in Indian, North African, Middle Eastern and Mexican cooking. It has a distinctive warm, savoury flavour, which is excellent in curries, couscous, poultry and meat stews. Seeds can be used whole, or ground in a mortar just before use.

Curry Powder

May be a strong or mild mixture of ground spices. There is no one specific blend – each powder is mixed according to taste and is based on spices native to India such as cinnamon, cloves, pepper, coriander, cumin, chillies and turmeric.

Fennel

Has been used as a herb and spice for thousands of years. The seeds have a warm fragrant flavour with a strong taste of anise. For years fennel has been used to enhance the flavour of fresh fish, in pickles and as an important ingredient in Indian vegetarian dishes.

Galangal

Native to Indonesia and southern China and closely related to the ginger family. It is a knobbly root which comes in two types: lesser and greater. Lesser galangal tastes like cardamom and ginger; greater galangal is similar to a mixture of ginger and pepper. Lesser galangal is used as a vegetable in southeast Asia, whilst greater galangal, available fresh, dried or ground, is used in curries, stews and coconut-based sauces. When unobtainable, you can substitute fresh root ginger. Store fresh galangal in a plastic bag in the refrigerator, dried galangal in an airtight container in a cool, dark place.

Garam Masala

A traditional spice mixture from Northern India (masala means 'mixture of spices'). There are literally hundreds of different masalas, each made from a combination of herbs and spices (cumin, coriander seeds, cinnamon, mace, cardamom, black peppercorns and bay leaf, for example). Other masalas based on pepper and cloves are much hotter. Use garam masala sparingly to flavour pilafs, birianis and meat dishes or sprinkle on food before serving.

Ginger

A knobbly root used extensively in most Asian cuisines where it is considered almost as important as salt. It is a versatile spice with a clean, fresh taste and is used to enhance the flavours of sweet and savoury dishes. Choose firm roots and keep wrapped in a paper towel in a plastic bag, in the refrigerator.

Mustard

A hot spice which derives from the cabbage family. White mustard seeds are used as a pickling spice and brown mustard seeds are an important flavouring in Indian cooking.

Nutmeg and Mace

Myristica fragrans is a unique plant because it produces two different spices under one shell. Mace is the lacy covering that surrounds the seed (the nutmeg) inside the shell. Nutmeg and mace have similar aromas and flavours although mace is slightly more refined. Nutmeg is used in sauces, custards and with vegetables and stewed fruits, whilst mace is used to flavour soups, sauces, fish and poultry dishes, cakes, desserts and custards. Freshly grated nutmeg has infinitely more flavour than ready ground.

Paprika

Made from ground dried sweet peppers. Originally from Mexico, the plants found their way to Hungary where paprika soon became an essential part of the local cuisine. Paprika has a lightly pungent, sweet flavour and is used in a wide variety of dishes including stews, soups and cream-based sauces. Paprika loses its flavour and aroma quickly, so buy in small quantities.

Poppy Seeds

Native to the Middle East, these are the ripe seeds of the opium poppy. They have a nutty, aroma and texture which is vastly improved by toasting. Delicious in breads, biscuits and cakes, curries and sauces. Grind the seeds in a mortar or coffee grinder.

Saffron

More than 250,000 hand-picked crocus flowers are used to make a pound of saffron – which explains why saffron is so expensive! Used as a spice since the 10th century, it is produced mostly in Spain. Saffron threads (the deeper the colour, the better the quality) are highly aromatic and preferable to ground saffron which quickly loses its flavour. It has a strong yellow colour and is indispensable in many sauces, stews and fish dishes such as bouillabaisse and paella. Buy in small quantities because saffron quickly loses its flavour.

Salt

Once valued so highly that is was used as an offering to God, today it is a relatively cheap commodity and its role decidedly more practical! It is used to season and preserve food, but also acts as a precious nutrient for the body. There are two types of salt: rock salt and sea salt. Sea salt is definitely more powerful than rock salt so use carefully. To prevent dampness, mix a few grains of rice with salt.

Sesame Seeds

These come in three varieties: white, brown or black. They contain 50 per cent oil and have a lovely nutty flavour that is enhanced by toasting (see page 14). Sesame seeds add a crunchy texture to sweet and savoury dishes, such as breads, cakes and biscuits or rice, vegetables and salad dressings.

Star Anise

A small, star-shaped fruit which has the aroma and flavour of anise. It is used extensively in Chinese and Vietnamese cooking and is an essential ingredient in Chinese five-spice powder. Star anise will keep indefinitely in an airtight container away from the light. Grind in a mortar or coffee grinder.

Tamarind

Has been cultivated in India for centuries and was probably brought to Europe in the 15th century by the Crusaders. It has a slightly sour, fruity flavour, with a pleasant, sweet aroma, and is used in India to flavour curries, vegetable stews and chutneys, or in any recipe needing a slight sourness. Tamarind concentrate is difficult to find but is more economical than fresh. Store in a plastic bag in the refrigerator.

Turmeric

A member of the ginger family which has been cultivated for thousands of years in tropical areas. Dried or ground, turmeric is an important ingredient in curry powders. It is also used to flavour pickles and many Indian vegetarian dishes. Turmeric can be used as a substitute for saffron, but although similar in colour it does not have the same, pungent flavour.

HOW TO

Toast nuts, seeds and coconut Toss them around in a hot, dry frying pan until they are lightly browned. Be careful not to burn them.

Skin tomatoes Put the tomatoes in a large bowl of boiling water and leave to stand for 1-2 minutes. Remove, and the skin will peel off easily.

Skin peppers and chillies Put them under the grill, skin side up, until the skins blister and go black. Then remove and pop them straight into a plastic bag. Allow to cool, then skin.

Reconstitute dried chillies Soak them in hot water for 20 minutes, then chop, shred or purée according to the type of chilli and recipe instructions.

THE RECIPES

SAUCES

All recipes are for four people.

SPICY CHICK PEA SAUCE MEDIUM-HOT

This sauce is delicious served with naan bread or as a side dish with curry. Good with merguez sausages.

3 cloves garlic, peeled
5 cm (2 inch) piece fresh root ginger,
peeled and roughly chopped
1 fresh medium-hot red chilli,
or 1 dried guajillo chilli, soaked,
puréed and sieved (see page 11)
1 teaspoon cumin seeds

1 teaspoon garam masala
2 tablespoons sunflower oil
1 red onion, chopped
400 g (14 oz) canned chick peas, with their
juice, roughly chopped in the blender
3 tablespoons fresh coriander, chopped
Salt and freshly ground black pepper

Place the garlic, ginger, chilli, cumin and garam masala in the blender and roughly chop for a few seconds.

Heat the oil in a heavy-based pan over a moderate heat, stir in the mixture and gently warm through. Add the onion and cook for 2 minutes, then add the chick peas and simmer for 10 minutes. Stir in the coriander and season to taste.

• If the mixture gets too thick, add a little more water.

LEMON AND CASHEW SAUCE

MILD AND AROMATIC

A delicate, slightly aromatic sauce. Serve stirred into wild or basmati rice.

100 g (4 oz) cashew nuts, toasted (see page 14)
and roughly chopped in the blender
1 teaspoon mustard seeds
1/2 teaspoon turmeric
Juice of 3 lemons

Grated rind of 2 lemons
1 teaspoon dried curry leaf, chopped
2 tablespoons sherry
1 teaspoon honey
Salt and freshly ground black pepper

Place the cashew nuts and mustard seeds in a hot pan and dry toast over a moderate heat for 4-6 minutes or until they brown slightly. Shake the pan frequently.

Add the rest of the ingredients and bring to the boil.

Season to taste and serve.

NEW ORLEANS RED BEAN SAUCE

MEDIUM-HOT

This is a traditional Cajun dish. Serve with bowls of fluffy white rice.

3 tablespoons extra virgin olive oil
6 cloves garlic, peeled and chopped
4 tomatoes, chopped
1 red pepper, chopped
15 okra, sliced into 5 mm (1/4 inch) rounds

2 bay leaves
1 tablespoon hot West Indian pepper sauce
400 g (14 oz) canned red kidney beans
with their juice
Salt and freshly ground black pepper

Heat the oil in a heavy-based pan over a moderate heat and gently sauté the garlic for 1-2 minutes. Add the tomatoes, red pepper, okra, bay leaves and hot pepper sauce and cook for 5 minutes.

Add the beans and simmer for a further 5 minutes.

Season and serve.

GUJARATI VEGETABLE AND BEAN SAUCE MEDIUM-HOT

A robust, gutsy sauce based on an authentic Indian recipe. Serve with rice or barbecued chicken.

2-3 tablespoons sunflower oil
2 fresh medium-hot green chillies,
finely chopped, or 2 dried guindilla chillies,
soaked, puréed and sieved (see page 11)
1 teaspoon turmeric
1 teaspoon black mustard seeds
1 teaspoon cumin seeds
5 cm (2 inch) piece fresh root ginger,
peeled and chopped

400 g (14 oz) canned yellow split peas
with their juice
200 g (7 oz) canned brown lentils
with their juice
200 g (7 oz) canned black eyed beans
1/2 aubergine, finely chopped (not skinned)
1/2 red pepper, finely chopped
Juice of 1 lime
Salt and freshly ground black pepper

Heat the oil in a heavy-based pan over a moderate heat, add the chillies, turmeric, mustard seeds, cumin seeds and ginger and gently warm through for 1-2 minutes, taking care not to burn.

Add the split peas, lentils, beans and vegetables. Bring to the boil, and simmer for 8 minutes.

Stir in the lime juice and season to taste.

• To make this sauce into a delicious soup, add 600 ml (1 pint) of fresh stock (available from supermarkets).

Right: *Persian Sauce*

PERSIAN SAUCE AROMATIC AND SPICY

Bursting with exotic Middle Eastern flavours and aromas, this pungent sauce is excellent on its own or mixed with rice.

4 cardamom pods
1/2 level teaspoon cloves, ground
1/2 teaspoon caraway seeds
5 saffron strands
2 tablespoons shelled pistachio nuts
1 tablespoon slivered almonds, toasted (see page 14)
6 fresh dates, stoned

2 tablespoons dried apricots, chopped, or zaradaloo (Middle Eastern dried apricots with honey), chopped
1 tablespoon Pernod
Pips of 1 pomegranate
Juice of 2 oranges
2 tablespoons water

Put all the ingredients, except the Pernod, pomegranate pips, orange juice and water in the food processor and blend for a few seconds.

Transfer the mixture to a bowl and stir in the water, Pernod, orange juice and pomegranate pips.

INDONESIAN COCONUT SAUCE

MILD AND AROMATIC

This is a wonderful Indonesian recipe. Mix with boiled white or Thai fragrant rice. Alternatively, try it with grilled fish or prawns, or cook the fish in the sauce.

2.5 cm (1 inch) piece dried galangal, grated
5 cm (2 inch) piece fresh root ginger, peeled and chopped
Flesh (and juice) of 1 coconut, chopped or 120 ml (4 fl oz) canned coconut milk

12 fennel seeds
150 ml (5 f l oz) water
1 tablespoon fresh coriander, chopped
Juice of 1/2 lime
Salt and freshly ground black pepper

Put the galangal, ginger, coconut, fennel seeds and half the water in a food processor and blend to a liquid paste. Then, with the motor still running, add the rest of the water.

Transfer the mixture to a saucepan and, over a moderate heat, slowly bring to the boil. Remove from the heat and stir in the coriander and lime juice.

Season to taste.

SAG DHAL VERY HOT

Serve with flat Indian bread such as chapati or boiled salad potatoes, or as an accompaniment to korma dishes. On its own, Sag Dhal makes a wonderful vegetable dish.

6 cloves garlic, peeled
2 fresh very hot green chillies, or 1 dried habañero chilli, soaked (see page 11), or 5 dried bird's eye chillies, crushed
5 cm (2 inch) piece fresh root ginger, peeled
3 tablespoons olive oil
1 teaspoon cumin seeds
12 cardamom pods

1 teaspoon mild curry powder
400 g (14 oz) canned green or brown lentils, drained
150 ml (5 fl oz) water
225 g (8 oz) fresh young spinach
Fresh coriander leaves
Salt and freshly ground black pepper

Put the garlic, chillies and ginger in the blender and grind until a smooth paste is formed.

Heat the oil in a heavy-based pan and cook the paste with the cumin seeds, cardamom pods and curry powder for 3-4 minutes.

Add the lentils, water and spinach and bring to the boil. Simmer for 2-3 minutes.

Transfer the mixture to a food processor and blend until smooth. Sprinkle with coriander and season to taste.

• To cool the sauce down add a little plain yoghurt.

GREEN MEXICAN SAUCE HOT AND SOUR

This is a typical Mexican sauce. Serve with tortillas or beef hash, or stirred into rice.

1 stick celery, roughly chopped
1 small onion, roughly chopped
2 green peppers, roughly chopped
6 cloves garlic, peeled and roughly chopped
3 fresh hot green chillies, deseeded, or 1 dried pasado chilli, soaked (see page 11) and roughly chopped

2 tablespoons oil
6 tablespoons fresh coriander, chopped
1 teaspoon ground cumin
1 teaspoon mixed dried herbs
Juice of 1 lime
150 ml (5 fl oz) water
Salt and freshly ground black pepper

Put the celery, onion, peppers, garlic and chillies in a food processor and blend until finely chopped.

Heat the oil in a heavy-based pan and fry the chopped vegetables for 3-4 minutes or until soft.

Add the coriander, cumin, mixed herbs, lime juice and water, heat through and stir together well.

Season to taste.

Left: Spicy Chick Pea Sauce

GREEN LENTIL DHAL HOT

Serve with Indian flat breads such as chapatis, with rice, or to accompany curry. Alternatively Green Lentil Dhal makes an excellent dish on its own.

4 cloves garlic, peeled and chopped	*2 tablespoons fresh coriander, chopped*
225 g (8 oz) onion, chopped	*1 tablespoon garam masala*
2 fresh bird's eye chillies, chopped,	*6 cardamom pods*
or 2 dried bird's eye chillies, soaked	*400 g (14 oz) canned green lentils*
and chopped	*with their juice*
3 tablespoons olive oil	*Salt and freshly ground black pepper*

Put the garlic, onion and chillies in a food processor and chop finely.

Heat the oil in a heavy-based pan over a moderate heat and fry the processed mixture for 2-3 minutes. Add the remaining ingredients and simmer for 10 minutes.

Season to taste.

• If the sauce is too thick add a little water.

• To make a lovely, gutsy soup add 600 ml (1 pint) of chicken stock.

PEPPER SAUCE MILD

A delicious combination of tomatoes, chillies, sweet peppers and fresh herbs. Mix the sauce with green beans or white cannellini beans, or toss with hot pasta.

2 tablespoons olive oil	*1 red pepper, cut into 5 mm*
4 cloves garlic, peeled and chopped	*(¹/₄ inch) dice*
¹/₂ onion, chopped	*1 large ripe tomato, chopped*
1 fresh mild red chilli, chopped, or	*3 tablespoons fresh basil, chopped,*
1 dried ancho chilli (no need to	*or 200 g (7 oz) canned chopped tomatoes*
soak), chopped	*3 tablespoons fresh oregano, chopped*
1 yellow pepper, cut into 5 mm	*Salt and freshly ground black pepper*
(¹/₄ inch) dice	

Heat the oil in a heavy-based pan and sauté the garlic, onion and chilli for 1-2 minutes. Add the peppers, tomato and herbs and simmer for a further 8-10 minutes or until the peppers are soft.

Transfer the mixture to a food processor and blend for 30 seconds. Season and serve.

SPICED BULGAR WHEAT MILD

Much more than a sauce, this is a meal on its own! Alternatively serve over a platter of cooked black beans.

100 g (4 oz) bulgar wheat	*1 teaspoon ground cumin*
600 ml (1 pint) boiling water	*¹/₂ teaspoon caraway seeds*
4 tablespoons olive oil	*¹/₂ teaspoon fennel seeds*
1 red pepper, chopped	*Pinch of ground cloves*
Juice and grated rind of 1 lemon	*1 tablespoon fresh flat leaf parsley, chopped*
2 cloves garlic, peeled and chopped	*Salt and freshly ground black pepper*

Simmer the bulgar wheat in the boiling water for 10-15 minutes. Drain and set aside.

Heat the oil in a heavy-based pan and sauté the pepper, lemon, garlic, cumin, caraway seeds, fennel seeds and cloves for 2-3 minutes. Then remove from the heat and stir in the bulgar wheat and parsley. Season and serve.

This makes an excellent cold dish, too.

HOT PEPPER VINAIGRETTE HOT

This is a wonderfully light, tangy dressing. Serve with cold green beans, a mushroom salad or artichoke hearts, or tossed with cold pasta.

4 tablespoons extra virgin olive oil	*2 tablespoons tomato purée*
1 tablespoon white wine vinegar	*4 drops Tabasco sauce*
1 teaspoon Dijon mustard	*Salt and freshly ground black pepper*
2 tablespoons sun-dried tomato paste	

Put all the ingredients in a bowl and mix together well.

CAJUN PEPPER JELLY MILD-MEDIUM

A lovely, colourful jelly. Just the thing to accompany lamb, beef, ham, bacon or parcels of cheese wrapped in filo pastry.

450 g (1 lb) redcurrant or quince jelly	*1 sachet powdered gelatin, dissolved in*
1 tablespoon mixed peppercorns, ground	*3 tablespoons hot water (not boiling)*

In a saucepan over a moderate heat melt the jelly. Stir in the peppercorns, then pour the liquid jelly into a bowl and place in the fridge to cool for 2 hours or until it has set. Spoon into a bowl and serve.

AUBERGINE AND MINT SAUCE COOL

A refreshing, minty sauce and a tasty dish on its own, too. Serve with toasted pitta bread, over a tomato salad or boiled or steamed potatoes, or as an accompaniment to lamb or beef curry.

Preheat the oven to 200°C/400°F/Gas 6.

1 aubergine	*1 teaspoon ground cinnamon*
2 tablespoons fresh mint, chopped	*Salt and freshly ground black pepper*
1 teaspoon sugar	

Place the aubergine on a small baking tray and cook in the oven for about 1 hour or until soft.

Remove from the oven and cool for a few minutes, then scoop out the flesh into a small bowl. Discard the skin. Using a fork, mash the flesh into a purée.

Put all the ingredients (including the aubergine) in a bowl and mix together well. Season to taste.

• Serve hot or cold.

SPICED HERB DRESSING SPICY

Bursting with flavour this gutsy sauce will spike up any salad, vegetable or rice dish.

2 tablespoons fresh basil leaves, chopped	*1 teaspoon cumin seeds*
2 tablespoons fresh tarragon leaves	*120 ml (4 fl oz) light olive oil*
2 tablespoons fresh parsley, chopped	*Grated rind and juice of 1/2 lemon*
2 tablespoons fresh chives, chopped	*1/4 teaspoon salt*
1 teaspoon fennel seeds	*Freshly ground black pepper*

Put all the ingredients in a bowl and mix together well. Season to taste with pepper.

POPPY SEED DRESSING MILD

This dressing has a mild, piquant flavour. Delicious with a green leaf, raw carrot or Chinese noodle salad.

4 tablespoons sunflower oil	*2 tablespoons poppy seeds*
4 tablespoons orange juice	*1/4 teaspoon salt*
1 teaspoon grated orange rind	*1/4 teaspoon freshly ground black pepper*

Put all the ingredients in a screw-top jar and shake well.

LOVAGE AND LIME SAUCE MILD

Simple to make, this sauce perfectly complements a fresh green or hot potato salad.

1 tablespoon fresh mint, chopped	*4 tablespoons sunflower oil*
1 tablespoon fresh coriander, chopped	*1 tablespoon lime juice*
1 tablespoon fresh lovage or celery	*1/2 teaspoon Dijon mustard*
leaves, chopped	*1/4 teaspoon salt*
1 fresh green chilli, finely chopped	*1/4 teaspoon freshly ground black pepper*

Put all the ingredients in a food processor and blend until finely chopped.

HOT BASIL DRESSING MEDIUM

Try this fresh-flavoured, nutty dressing over hot or cold Chinese noodles, grilled tomatoes, whole globe artichokes, broccoli or cauliflower.

4 tablespoons fresh basil, chopped	*2 tablespoons sunflower oil*
2 tablespoons walnut pieces	*Juice of 1/2 lemon*
1 fresh medium green chilli, or	*1/4 teaspoon salt*
1/2 dried pasilla chilli, soaked	*1/4 teaspoon freshly ground black pepper*
2 tablespoons walnut oil	

Put all the ingredients in a food processor and blend until finely chopped.

COCONUT AND CHILLI SAUCE
MEDIUM-HOT AND AROMATIC

A smooth, creamy sauce, delicious over hard-boiled eggs, mixed vegetables, mixed root vegetables or rice.

2 onions, quartered	*2 teaspoons garam masala or curry powder*
7.5 cm (3 inch) piece fresh root ginger,	*1/4 teaspoon salt*
peeled and cut into 2.5 cm (1 inch) slices	*1/4 teaspoon freshly ground black pepper*
2 fresh medium-hot green chillies, chopped,	*2 tablespoons groundnut oil*
or 2 dried guajillo chillies, soaked, puréed	*2 tablespoons sunflower oil*
and sieved (see page 11)	*400 g (14 oz) canned coconut milk*
5 cloves garlic, peeled	

Put all the ingredients, except the oils and coconut milk, into the food processor and blend until smooth. Heat the oils in a heavy-based pan over a moderate heat and sauté the processed mixture for 2 minutes, stirring continuously. Add the coconut milk and simmer for 5 minutes.

Season to taste.

Gado Gado Sauce MEDIUM-HOT

This is a hot, crunchy sauce which complements deep-fried bean curd, bean sprouts, pakchoy, and many other oriental vegetables to perfection. Alternatively, try it with a cold chicken salad.

2 tablespoons sesame oil	225 g (8 oz) peanuts, roasted
2 fresh medium-hot red chillies, chopped,	(see page 14) and crushed
or 1 dried cascabel chilli, soaked (see page 11),	150 ml (5 fl oz) water
flesh scooped out and puréed	Juice of 1 lime
2.5 cm (1 inch) fresh root ginger, chopped	Salt and freshly ground black pepper
	1 level teaspoon five spice powder

Heat the oil in a heavy-based pan over a moderate heat and sauté the chillies and ginger for 2 minutes. Add the peanuts and water and cook for a further 3-4 minutes. Then add the lime juice. Season, and stir in the five spice powder.

Black olive and chilli sauce

MEDIUM-HOT

A strong-tasting sauce which enhances the flavour of fried courgettes, stir fried aubergines and toasted goat's cheese.

1 red pepper, quartered	2 tablespoons black olive paste
1-2 fresh medium-hot red chillies,	4 tablespoons olive oil
halved and deseeded, or 1 dried ancho or	1 tablespoon balsamic vineger
chipotle chilli, soaked (see page 11)	Salt and freshly ground black pepper

Place the red pepper and chillies under a hot grill, skin side up, and cook until the skins blister and turn black, then transfer to a food processor. Add the rest of the ingredients and blend until smooth.

Season to taste.

Aioli MEDIUM-HOT

This popular sauce has a wonderful garlicky flavour. Try it with raw vegetables, grilled prawns or asparagus, or to flavour fish soup.

5 cloves garlic, peeled	Juice of 1/2 lemon
1/2 teaspoon salt	175-250 ml (6-8 fl oz) olive oil
2 egg yolks	Salt and freshly ground black pepper

Put the garlic and salt in a pestle and mortar and crush to a paste, then place in the food processor with the egg yolks and lemon juice and blend for 1 minute.

With the motor still running, slowly pour in the oil – too much too quickly will make the sauce curdle – until the mixture thickens.

Season to taste.

CORIANDER PISTOU SAUCE MILD

This aromatic sauce has a strong flavour. Serve with goat's cheese, stir into vegetable soup, or toss with pasta.

4 tablespoons fresh coriander, chopped
5 cloves garlic, peeled
5-6 tablespoons olive oil
Juice of 1/2 lemon
1/4 teaspoon salt
1/4 teaspoon freshly ground black pepper

Put all the ingredients in a food processor and blend until smooth.

HOT TOMATO AND CHILLI SAUCE HOT

This is mighty hot! Try this full-flavoured sauce with grilled courgettes, over globe artichokes, with seafood or focaccia bread.

2 heaped tablespoons sun-dried
tomato paste
2 hot fresh red chillies, or 1 dried
habañero chilli, soaked (see page 11)
2 tablespoons olive oil
Juice of 1/2 lemon
2 tablespoons red wine vinegar
Salt and freshly ground black pepper

Put all the ingredients in the food processor and blend until smooth.

Season to taste.

AROMATIC YOGHURT RHAITA COOL

Use this fresh, minty sauce to cool down curries, dhals or any hot dish.

2 tablespoons fresh mint, finely chopped
1/4 teaspoon salt
1/4 teaspoon freshly ground black pepper
150 ml (5 fl oz) plain yoghurt

Put all the ingredients in a bowl and mix together until smooth.

• Greek yoghurt will give the sauce a thicker, creamier texture.

SPICED LEMON DRESSING SPICY

This fresh, tangy sauce is perfection with asparagus, prawns and cold chicken.

2 lemons, peeled segments and grated rind
2.5 cm (1 inch) piece fresh root ginger, peeled
150 ml (5 fl oz) sunflower oil
Salt and freshly ground black pepper

Put all the ingredients in a food processor and blend until smooth.

Season to taste.

HORSERADISH CREAM MEDIUM-HOT

This is a hot sauce with a smooth, creamy texture. Delicious with beetroot, new potatoes, smoked salmon, peppered mackerel or cold beef.

150 ml (5 fl oz) whipping cream
5-7.5 cm (2-3 inch) or 150 g (5 oz) piece
fresh horseradish, peeled and grated
Pinch of grated lemon rind
1 teaspoon lemon juice
1 teaspoon Dijon mustard
1 tablespoon fresh chives, chopped
Salt and freshly ground black pepper

Whip the cream until thick, then stir in the rest of the ingredients and mix together well.

Season to taste.

CHILLI PEPPER SHERRY HOT

Quick and easy to make, chilli pepper sherry will definitely spike up any vegetable soup, broth or consommé. Excellent in stews, tomato juice and Bloody Marys too.

600 ml (1 pint) dry sherry
1 fresh hot green chilli, or 5 dried bird's eye chillies

Put the sherry and chilli in a clean bottle and leave to steep for 1 week.

Top up with more sherry and use sparingly.

• Chilli pepper sherry will keep for at least a year.

CHILLI OIL HOT

Hot chilli oil is simple to make and just the thing to liven up plain mayonnaise and salad dressings.

Small bottle extra virgin olive oil
12 small fresh hot red and green chillies,
scored all over with the tip of a knife,
or 12 dried bird's eye chillies

Put the oil and chillies in a sterilised bottle and leave to infuse for 2 weeks. Use sparingly.

• Keep in a cool place away from the light.

HOT MUSTARD AND HORSERADISH SAUCE HOT

Don't be under any illusion – this sauce is hot! Excellent with smoked fish or any raw fish or meat tartare.

7.5 cm (3 inch) piece, or about 4 tablespoons,
fresh horseradish, peeled and grated
1 large gherkin, about 7.5 cm (3 inches)
1 tablespoon capers
1 teaspoon dry mustard
1/2 teaspoon freshly ground black pepper
3 tablespoons thick cream or fromage blanc
Juice of 1 lemon

Put all the ingredients, except the cream and lemon juice in a food processor and blend until very finely chopped. Transfer the mixture to a bowl, and quickly stir in the cream and lemon juice – too much stirring can cause the sauce to curdle.

Right: Hot Pepper Vinaigrette

CUCUMBER AND GINGER SAUCE MEDIUM

This sauce has a lovely oriental flavour and is delicious with grilled swordfish, conger eel, monkfish and salmon.

2 cloves garlic, peeled and finely chopped
2 fresh medium-hot green chillies, finely chopped, or 2 dried pasado chillies, soaked (see page 11) and finely chopped
5 cm (2 inch) piece fresh root ginger, peeled and chopped
10 cm (4 inch) piece cucumber, chopped
200 ml (7 fl oz) rice vinegar
4 tablespoons soy sauce
50 g (2 oz) sesame seeds, toasted (see page 14)

Put all the ingredients in a bowl and mix together well.

RED CHILLI VELOUTE MEDIUM

This sauce is wonderful with clams and mussels. Alternatively, serve it with smoked haddock.

2 tablespoons olive oil or 25 g (1 oz) butter
2 cloves garlic, peeled and crushed
1 fresh medium-hot red chilli, finely chopped, or 1 dried ancho chilli, soaked (see page 11) and finely chopped
2 wineglasses white wine
4 spring onions, trimmed and chopped
3 heaped tablespoons crème fraîche
Salt and freshly ground black pepper
2 tablespoons fresh flat leaf parsley, chopped

Heat the oil in a heavy-based pan and gently sauté the garlic and chilli. Add the white wine, bring to the boil and simmer for 3-4 minutes.

Stir in the spring onions and cream and simmer for a further 1-2 minutes, then season and sprinkle with parsley.

• For a lovely smoky flavour use 2-3 dried chipotle chillies, soaked (see page 11) and puréed.

• To make a wonderful soup, pour the sauce into a deep-sided pan, add 2 wineglasses of white wine and bring to the boil. Throw in 1 kg (2 ¹/₂ lb) of well-scrubbed mussels, put on the lid and cook for 5 minutes or until the mussels are all open.

MALAYSIAN PICKLE SAUCE HOT

This sauce has a slightly crunchy texture and is a very good dish on its own. Excellent with raw or grilled fish, plus prawns and chicken.

¹/₂ turnip, grated
¹/₂ parsnip, grated
1 carrot, grated
3 tablespoons rice wine vinegar
Juice of 1 lime
2 teaspoons soy sauce
1 tablespoon sesame seeds, toasted (see page 14)
1 tablespoon peanuts, toasted (see page 14) and crushed in a food processor or coffee grinder
1 fresh hot red chilli, sliced and deseeded
Salt and freshly ground black pepper

Put all the ingredients in a bowl and mix together well.

Season to taste.

Right: New Orleans Red Bean Sauce

SPRING ONION SAUCE MEDIUM

Quick and easy to prepare, this sophisticated sauce is delicious with fish cakes and grilled white fish.

250 ml (8 fl oz) home-made or good	Freshly ground black pepper
quality ready-made mayonnaise	1/4 teaspoon caster sugar
3 tablespoons double cream	5 tablespoons spring onions,
2 teaspoons Tabasco sauce	trimmed and roughly chopped
Juice of 1/2 lemon	1 egg, hard boiled, chopped
1/4 teaspoon dried mustard	1 tablespoon parsley, chopped
1 teaspoon salt	1 teaspoon Worcestershire sauce

Put all the ingredients in a large bowl and mix together well.

SWEET PEPPER SAUCE MEDIUM

This colourful sauce not only looks good but tastes wonderful too. Try it with fish cakes, crab cakes or grilled goat's cheese served on a bed of lettuce.

1 tablespoon olive oil	1/2 teaspoon cayenne
15 g (1/2 oz) butter	3 tablespoons crème fraîche
3 red or yellow peppers, roughly chopped	Salt and freshly ground black pepper
3 cloves garlic, peeled and crushed	3 spring onions, finely chopped
2 teaspoons ground coriander	

Heat the oil and butter in a heavy-based pan over a low heat and gently sauté the peppers and garlic until soft. Add the coriander, cayenne, crème fraîche and seasoning and stir well.

Put the mixture in a food processor and blend until smooth, then transfer to a bowl and sprinkle with the spring onions.

AROMATIC FENNEL SAUCE SPICY

Simple to make, try this delicate, creamy sauce with a firm white fish such as sea bass, sole or turbot.

15 g (1/2 oz) butter	6 fennel seeds
1 tablespoon sunflower oil	1 teaspoon cumin seeds
1 fennel bulb, roughly chopped	4 tablespoons crème fraîche
3 tablespoons Pernod	Salt and freshly ground black pepper
1/2 teaspoon caraway seeds	2 tablespoons fresh flat leaf parsley, chopped

Melt the butter with the oil in a heavy-based pan over a low heat and gently sauté the fennel until soft but not brown.

Add the Pernod, then turn up the heat and stir in the caraway, fennel and cumin seeds. Simmer until 1/2 of the liquid has evaporated, then add the cream, bring to the boil and season to taste.

Transfer the mixture to a food processor and blend until smooth.

Sprinkle with parsley.

GREEN CHUTNEY SAUCE MEDIUM-HOT

A slightly sweet, piquant sauce. Wonderful with red mullet, grey mullet or any Pacific fish.

3 tablespoons oil	2 mangoes, flesh diced into 1.25 cm
1 teaspoon black mustard seeds	(1/2 inch) cubes
3 cloves garlic, peeled	2 tablespoons sherry
5 cm (2 inch) piece fresh root ginger, peeled	Juice of 1 lime
2 fresh medium-hot green chillies, or 1	1 tablespoon sugar
dried habañero chilli, soaked (see page 11)	2 tablespoons fresh coriander, chopped
2 tablespoons water	Salt and freshly ground black pepper

Heat the oil in a heavy-based pan over a moderate heat and cook the mustard seeds until they begin to 'pop'. Remove the pan from the heat and set aside.

Put the garlic, ginger, chillies and water in a food processor and blend until a smooth paste is formed. Transfer the paste to the pan and cook over a low heat for 5 minutes.

Stir in the mango cubes, sherry, lime juice and sugar and slowly heat through.

Sprinkle with the coriander, season and serve.

SPICED YOGHURT SAUCE COOL

A spicy yet cooling sauce for marinated fish or curry dishes. Alternatively, use as a dipping sauce for grilled prawns.

2 tablespoons sunflower oil	1/2 teaspoon cayenne
4 cloves garlic, peeled and chopped	1/2 teaspoon freshly ground black pepper
1 teaspoon turmeric	10 cardamom pods
1 teaspoon ground cinnamon	8 tablespoons Greek yoghurt
1 teaspoon cumin seeds	Salt and freshly ground black pepper
1 teaspoon fennel seeds	

Put the oil in a heavy-based pan and gently heat the garlic, turmeric, cinnamon, cumin seeds, fennel seeds, cayenne, black pepper and cardamom pods for 2-3 minutes.

Transfer the mixture to a food processor and blend until smooth, then return to the pan. Add the yoghurt and gently heat through.

Sieve the mixture to remove spice husks, then stir thoroughly.

Season and serve.

• This sauce makes an excellent marinade. Use exactly the same method but don't heat the yoghurt.

SWEET AND SOUR PEACH SAUCE MILD

As the name suggests this is a wonderful combination of sweet and sour ingredients. Excellent with lobster, gammon or red mullet.

2 tablespoons rice wine vinegar
2 tablespoons liquid honey
3 peaches, stones removed and finely sliced

1 fresh mild red chilli, finely chopped,
or 1 dried ancho chilli, soaked
(see page 11) and finely chopped
1/2 red onion, finely chopped
Salt and freshly ground black pepper

Put all the ingredients in a bowl and mix together well. Season to taste.

• Will keep for a week in the refrigerator.

JAFFA SAUCE MILD

An ingenious combination of ingredients especially created to complement Pacific fish such as tuna, swordfish, barracuda and parrot fish.

1 tablespoon olive oil
Rind of 1 orange, grated or cut
into fine strips
Juice of 2 oranges
1/3 cucumber, peeled, deseeded
and finely chopped

3 shallots, finely sliced
1/2 teaspoon poppy seeds
2 tablespoons fresh coriander, chopped
Salt and freshly ground black pepper

Put all the ingredients in a bowl and mix together well.

Season to taste.

MOROCCAN BLACK PEPPER SAUCE

HOT AND AROMATIC

This strong, gutsy sauce is based on a well-known traditional recipe. Delicious with grilled or steamed white fish such as halibut, monkfish, sea bass, cod, king or tiger prawns or scallops. Alternatively, it makes a good dipping sauce.

50 g (2 oz) butter or 4 tablespoons
sunflower oil
2 onions, finely chopped or grated
4 tablespoons fresh parsley, finely chopped
2 teaspoons ground black pepper

1/2 teaspoon cayenne
2 teaspoons ground cinnamon
600 ml (1 pint) Greek yoghurt
Pinch of salt

Heat the butter or oil in a heavy-based pan and gently fry the onions, parsley, black pepper, cayenne and cinnamon for 2-3 minutes, taking care not to burn them.

Stir in the yoghurt and salt, then quickly remove the pan from the heat – the spices will heat the yoghurt.

SPICED CUCUMBER SAUCE MILD

Based on an Indian recipe, this tasty sauce is delicious with fish such as barbecued or marinated tuna, grilled swordfish or prawns. It also makes an excellent cooler for curries and other hot dishes.

1/2 cucumber, deseeded and finely chopped
1/4 melon, skin removed, deseeded
and finely chopped
1 teaspoon ground coriander
1 tablespoon fresh mint, chopped

2 cloves garlic, peeled and crushed
or chopped
Salt and freshly ground black pepper
3 tablespoons olive oil
Juice of 1/2 lemon

Put all the ingredients in a bowl and mix thoroughly.

PARSLEY AND LEMON SAUCE MILD

Use this light, herby sauce to stuff sardines, or rolled plaice or sole, en papillote, or serve with steamed or grilled cod.

50 g (2 oz) fresh flat leaf parsley,
finely chopped
1 teaspoon ground white pepper
1/2 teaspoon salt

5 tablespoons sunflower oil
2 tablespoons olive oil
Juice and rind of 1 lemon

Place the parsley, pepper and salt in the food processor. Switch on the motor and slowly pour the oils into the mixture. Add the lemon rind and juice, then check the seasoning and serve.

CORIANDER AND GARLIC SAUCE

MILD AND AROMATIC

Bursting with flavour, this wonderfully aromatic sauce is perfection with grilled prawns, mussels, clams, squid or a mixed seafood salad.

2 tablespoons sunflower oil
2 tablespoons walnut or hazelnut oil
2 tablespoons lime juice
2 tablespoons fresh coriander, chopped

4 cloves garlic, peeled
1 teaspoon black pepper
Salt
2 tablespoons cream

Put all the ingredients in a food processor and blend until smooth.

Right: Lemon and Chilli Marinade

CARDAMOM SAUCE MEDIUM-HOT

This strong, spicy sauce complements grilled chicken breasts and lamb chops to perfection.

3 tablespoons sunflower oil
2.5 cm (1 inch) piece fresh root ginger, peeled and chopped
4 cloves garlic, peeled and crushed
1 teaspoon cardamom pods
1 teaspoon fennel seeds
1 teaspoon ground coriander
300 ml (10 fl oz) plain yoghurt
Salt

Put all the ingredients, except the yoghurt in a food processor and blend to a coarse paste. Transfer to a heavy-based pan and gently warm through. Stir in the yoghurt and bring to the boil. Season with salt and serve.

• Try cooking small pieces of raw chicken or lamb in the sauce: simmer for 30-40 minutes or until the meat is tender.
(Use milk instead of yoghurt, if preferred.)

CORIANDER AND HONEY SAUCE

MILD AND SPICY

The unusual combination of honey, coriander and citrus fruits is sweet and fresh. Serve over chicken breasts or roast duck.

25 g (1 oz) butter
2.5 cm (1 inch) piece fresh root ginger, peeled and cut into thin slices
1 teaspoon grated lemon rind
1 teaspoon grated orange rind
1/2 teaspoon ground cloves
1/2 teaspoon caraway seeds
6 cardamom pods
Juice of 1 orange
6 tablespoons liquid honey
2 tablespoons fresh coriander, finely chopped
Salt and freshly ground black pepper

Melt the butter in a heavy-based pan over a moderate heat. Add the ginger, lemon rind, orange rind, cloves, caraway seeds and cardamom pods and heat for 2-3 minutes, taking care not to burn them.

Stir in the orange juice and honey, then bring to the boil and simmer for 2 minutes.

Sprinkle with coriander, season and serve.

HOT CHILLI AND COCONUT SAUCE

HOT

This is an inspirational combination of mouthwatering ingredients, especially for lovers of hot food! Excellent with chicken and fish.

2 x 50 g (2 oz) sachets of creamed coconut
150 ml (5 fl oz) boiling water
6 fresh green Thai chillies, deseeded and finely chopped, or 2 dried habañero chillies, soaked (see page 11) and finely chopped
2 tablespoons fresh coriander, chopped
1 tablespoon ground cumin
2.5 cm (1 inch) piece fresh root ginger, peeled and chopped
1 onion, finely chopped
3 cloves garlic, peeled
1 teaspoon ground black pepper
Grated rind of 1/2 lemon
1 tablespoon fresh lime juice
2 stalks lemon grass, topped, tailed and tough outer leaves removed
1 teaspoon coriander seeds, crushed
1 tablespoon groundnut oil
375 ml (13 fl oz) hot water
1 lime, sliced

Whisking with a fork, dissolve the creamed coconut in the boiling water and set aside to cool.

Put the remaining ingredients, except the lime slices, in the food processor and blend until smooth, then transfer the mixture to a bowl and stir in the creamed coconut.

Decorate with slices of lime.

ANDALUSIAN SAUCE MEDIUM-HOT

This is a fairly robust sauce. Serve with boiled gammon or bacon joints, pork or chicken breasts.

4 cloves garlic, peeled and chopped
1 red onion, quartered
1 fresh medium-hot red chilli, or 1 dried guindilla chilli, soaked, puréed and sieved (see page 11)
4 tablespoons fresh mint, chopped
3 tablespoons olive oil
225 g (8 oz) smoked ham, chopped into small pieces
400 g (14 oz) canned green lentils, with the juice
Pinch of saffron threads
Salt and freshly ground black pepper
150 ml (5 fl oz) water

Place the garlic, onion, chilli and mint in a food processor and blend until finely chopped.

Heat the oil in a wok or deep-sided pan and stir-fry the processed mixture with the ham for 1-2 minutes.

Add the lentils, saffron, salt and a little more water if the sauce is too dry and simmer for 5-6 minutes.

Season to taste.

• To make a richly flavoured soup add 600 ml (1 pint) of fresh stock (available from supermarkets).

Right: Green Chutney Sauce

Above: Sweet and Sour Peach Sauce

THAI RED CURRY SAUCE HOT

Red and green Thai sauces can be used to flavour or accompany a wide variety of dishes and ingredients. Serve over beef, chicken, prawns, monkfish or vegetables. Alternatively use as a side sauce for grilled chicken. (See also Green Thai Sauce.)

1 tablespoon sunflower oil
2 tablespoons red curry paste
400 g (14 oz) canned coconut milk

4-8 baby aubergines, whole or halved depending on their size

Heat the oil in a heavy-based pan and gently fry the curry paste for 1-2 minutes. Then add the coconut milk and aubergines and simmer for 10-15 minutes.

THAI GREEN CURRY SAUCE HOT

Thai Green Curry Sauce has a slightly sour taste which complements vegetables, beef, chicken and prawns to perfection.

1 tablespoon sunflower oil
2 tablespoons green curry paste
400 g (14 oz) canned coconut milk

4-8 baby aubergines, whole or halved depending on their size

Heat the oil in a heavy-based pan and gently fry the paste for 1-2 minutes. Then add the coconut milk and aubergines and simmer for 10-15 minutes.

• Cook thin strips of beef, or small pieces of chicken prawns or vegetables in the sauce.

PINEAPPLE AND CASHEW SAUCE MILD

This is a tangy, full-bodied sauce with a sweet, spicy flavour. Try it with barbecued marinated chicken.

225 g (8 oz) canned or fresh, ripe pineapple, drained and crushed
1 stalk lemon grass, topped, tailed and tough outer leaves removed
1 clove garlic, peeled
6 shallots, roughly chopped
2-3 dried chipotle chillies, soaked (see page 11)
100 g (4 oz) unsalted macadamia nuts
2 tablespoons groundnut oil

225 g (8 oz) canned coconut milk
1 tablespoon tamarind pulp, soaked in water, then drained and sieved
2 tablespoons unsalted cashew nuts, toasted (see page 11)
1 teaspoon soft brown sugar
1 tablespoon soy sauce
Salt and freshly ground black pepper

Place the crushed pineapple in a bowl and set aside.

Put the lemon grass, garlic, shallots, chillies and nuts in the food processor and blend for 1-2 minutes or until a smooth paste is formed.

Heat the oil in a heavy-based saucepan and fry the paste for 3-4 minutes, stirring constantly.

Add the coconut milk and bring the mixture to the boil, then simmer for 30 seconds, stirring all the time.

Add the remaining ingredients and simmer for a further 5 minutes. Put the mixture into a bowl and allow to cool at room temperature.

Season and stir in the pineapple just before serving.

TOMATO CATSUP MILD

This is the real thing! Use this tasty sauce to pep up barbecued or chargrilled chicken, burgers and beef hash.

1 tablespoon olive oil
1 large onion, very finely chopped
6 very ripe tomatoes, deseeded and roughly chopped, or 400 g (14 oz) canned chopped Italian tomatoes
50 g (2 oz) brown sugar or black treacle
25 g (1 oz) white sugar

1 teaspoon salt
1/2 teaspoon black pepper
1/4 teaspoon ground allspice
4 tablespoons malt vinegar
1 tablespoon tomato purée
Juice of 1/2 lemon
Salt and freshly ground black pepper

Heat the oil in a deep-sided pan and, when it begins to smoke, throw in the onion and tomatoes and put on the lid. Let the tomatoes bubble furiously and when they calm down, remove the lid and add the rest of the ingredients, except the lemon juice.

Lower the heat and cook uncovered for 30 minutes, stirring occasionally. Add a little water if the liquid evaporates too much during the cooking process.

Remove the pan from the heat and add the lemon juice, then transfer the mixture to a food processor and blend until smooth.

Season to taste.

• Sieve for best results.

Spiced quince sauce MILD

The sweet and sour combination of quince and chillies makes this an ideal sauce to serve with roast partridge, roast pork or duck breasts.

1 stick celery, finely diced
3 quinces or pears, peeled,
cored and finely diced
1 fresh mild green chilli, finely diced,
or 1 dried pasado chilli, soaked
(see page 11) and finely diced

2 cloves garlic, peeled and finely chopped
1 tablespoon honey
2 tablespoons white wine vinegar
1 tablespoon lemon juice
Salt

Put all the ingredients in a pan, then bring to the boil and simmer for 1 minute.

Transfer the mixture to a bowl and stir well.

• This sauce can be served hot or cold.

Peppered parsley sauce MEDIUM

This fresh, highly seasoned sauce is excellent with roast fillet of beef, ham, cod steaks and monkfish.

50 g (2 oz) fresh parsley, chopped
Grated rind of 1 lemon
Juice of 2 lemons
1 small onion, quartered
6 tablespoons olive oil
1 tablespoon dry mustard

1 tablespoon capers
1 gherkin – about 7.5 cm (3 inches)
1/2 teaspoon freshly ground black pepper
1/2 teaspoon cayenne
Salt and freshly ground black pepper

Put all the ingredients in a food processor and blend until finely chopped.

Season to taste.

Sweet pickled sauce MEDIUM

The sharp, slightly tangy flavour of this delicious sauce works well with baked ham, sausages, black pudding and cheese.

300 ml (10 fl oz) water
600 ml (1 pint) malt vinegar
Pinch of salt
100 g (4 oz) cauliflower florets
10 pickling onions
1/2 green pepper, cut into 5 cm
(1/4 inch) dice
1 gherkin, chopped

1 teaspoon yellow mustard seeds
1 teaspoon green peppercorns in brine,
drained and slightly crushed
1 tablespoon dry mustard
1 tablespoon sunflower oil
1 tablespoon caster sugar
Salt and freshly ground black pepper

Put the water, vinegar and salt in a pan and bring to the boil. Add the cauliflower, pickling onions and green peppercorns and cook for 5 minutes, then drain, retaining 5 tablespoons of the liquid.

Put the remaining ingredients in a bowl, add the reserved cooking liquid and cooked vegetables and mix together well. Season to taste.

Black bean sauce VERY HOT

This powerful sauce is not for the faint hearted! Excellent with beef hash or burgers.

2-3 tablespoons sunflower oil
2 fresh habañero chillies, or 3 dried
habañero chillies, soaked (see page 11)
4 cloves garlic, peeled
4 tomatoes, deseeded and chopped

450 g (1 lb) canned black beans, drained,
or 225 g (8 oz) black beans, soaked in water
overnight, then drained and cooked
until soft but not mushy
3 tablespoons fresh coriander, chopped
Salt and freshly ground black pepper

Put the oil, chillies and garlic in a food processor and blend until smooth.

Transfer the mixture to heavy-based pan, add the tomatoes and cook over a moderate heat for 3 minutes.

Add the beans and cook for a further 3 minutes.

Stir in the coriander, season and serve.

SPICE ISLAND SAUCE MEDIUM-HOT

As its name suggests this sauce has a pungent, spicy flavour. Delicious with black eyed or borlotti beans. Alternatively, try it with polenta.

4 rashers smoked back bacon, rind removed
4 cloves garlic, peeled
1/2 white onion
2 fresh medium-hot red chillies, or 1 dried cascabel chilli, soaked (see page 11)
1 teaspoon dried marjoram
1 level teaspoon medium curry powder
1/2 teaspoon fennel seeds
1 tablespoon green peppercorns in brine, drained and slightly crushed
225 g (8 oz) sun-dried tomatoes, drained of oil
6 fresh tomatoes, chopped or 400 g (14 oz) canned chopped Italian tomatoes
Salt and freshly ground black pepper

Put all the ingredients, except the fresh tomatoes, in a food processor and blend until finely chopped, then transfer the mixture to a heavy-based pan. Sauté for 4-5 minutes.

Add the fresh tomatoes and simmer for a further 10 minutes. Season and serve.

GREEN PEPPERCORN SAUCE MEDIUM

AND SPICY

This is a sophisticated sauce with an unusual texture. Serve over roast duck breasts, medallions of veal or a fillet of beef.

20 g (3/4 oz) butter
20 g (3/4 oz) sugar
2 apples, peeled, cored and cut into
8 segments each
4 tablespoons white vermouth
175 ml (6 fl oz) fresh vegetable or poultry stock (available in supermarkets)
2-3 tablespoons double cream
20 g (3/4 oz) green peppercorns in brine, drained and crushed
Salt and freshly ground black pepper

Melt the butter and sugar in a heavy-based pan over a moderate heat and sauté the apple segments for 2-3 minutes.

Using a slotted spoon, transfer the apples to a bowl and and set aside.

Add the vermouth and stock to the pan and simmer for 3-4 minutes or until the mixture reduces a little. Then add the cream and cook for a further 3-4 minutes.

Return the apples to the pan, add the peppercorns and stir together well. Season to taste.

SWEET AND SOUR SESAME SAUCE MILD

Sweet yet sour, with a lovely crunchy texture, this is an ideal sauce to serve with crispy roast duck or grilled chicken or as a dish on the side.

3 tablespoons redcurrant jelly
2 tablespoons soy sauce
150 ml (5 fl oz) water
1 teaspoon fresh root ginger, finely chopped
1 small fresh mild red chilli, deseeded and chopped
1/2 cucumber, peeled, deseeded and chopped
4 spring onions, sliced
1 tablespoon sesame seeds, toasted (see page 14)

Put the redcurrant jelly, soy sauce, water, ginger and chilli in a saucepan and bring to the boil, then lower the heat and simmer for 5 minutes, stirring occasionally.

Add the cucumber, spring onions and sesame seeds and stir thoroughly. Remove the mixture from the heat and serve.

CHILLI AIOLI HOT

Excellent with crudités, grilled fish, prawns and lamb kebabs.

3 (or more if preferred) fresh hot red chillies, or 2 tablespoons Pimenton de la Vera chilli powder
3 cloves garlic, peeled
1/2 teaspoon freshly ground black pepper
3 egg yolks
200 ml (7 fl oz) olive oil, or 120 ml (4 fl oz) and 85 ml (3 fl oz) sunflower oil
Juice of 1/2 lemon
Salt and freshly ground black pepper.

Put the chillies (or chilli powder) and garlic in a food processor and blend for 30 seconds, then add the black pepper and egg yolks.

With the motor still running, slowly pour in three-quarters of the oil, then turn off the processor, add a teaspoon of lemon juice and taste. Keep adding the lemon juice, a teaspoon at a time, until the desired sharpness is acquired, then slowly pour in the rest of the oil.

Season to taste.

Right: Black Bean Sauce

Sherry and Garlic Sauce AROMATIC

This rich, warm sauce is the perfect accompaniment to home-made meatballs. Alternatively, try it with pan-fried chicken or pork chops.

1 fresh green chilli, roughly chopped,
or 1 dried guajillo chilli, soaked
(see page 11), puréed and sieved
2 cloves garlic, peeled and roughly chopped
1 rasher smoked bacon, rind removed,
cut into pieces

1 tablespoon olive oil
1 wineglass dry sherry
3 tablespoons crème fraîche
2-3 threads saffron
Salt and freshly ground black pepper
1 tablespoon fresh mint leaves, chopped

Put the chilli, garlic and bacon in the food processor and blend until finely chopped.

Heat the oil in a heavy-based pan over a moderate heat and sauté the processed mixture for 2-3 minutes, then add the sherry and bring to the boil. Simmer for 1-2 minutes. Add the crème fraîche and saffron and simmer for a further 2 minutes.

Season and sprinkle with mint.

Neapolitan Sweet Pepper Sauce

MEDIUM-HOT

Bursting with Mediterranean flavours and aromas, this wonderful sauce is delicious with beefburgers, meat pâtés, sausages and meat loaves.

4 tablespoons olive oil
4 rashers smoked bacon or pancetta,
any rind removed, roughly chopped
1 red onion, quartered
4 cloves garlic, peeled
1 fresh hot green chilli, or 2 dried guajillo
chillies, soaked, puréed and sieved (see page11)

2 red peppers, roughly chopped
3 tomatoes, quartered
1 wineglass white wine
1 tablespoon fresh parsley, chopped
Salt and freshly ground black pepper

Put the oil, bacon, onion, garlic and green chilli in a food processor and blend until finely chopped.

Transfer the mixture to a heavy-based pan, and cook over a moderate heat for 2-3 minutes.

Add the red peppers, tomatoes and wine and simmer for 10 minutes.

Stir in the parsley and season to taste.

Left: Green Peppercorn Sauce

DIPS

All recipes are for four people.

LIME PICKLE DIP HOT

The inspired combination of hot pickle, yoghurt and fresh coriander is highly recommended! Serve with cheese, ham, vegetables or skewered chicken.

225 g (8 oz) hot lime pickle
300 ml (10 fl oz) plain Greek yoghurt

1 tablespoon fresh coriander, chopped

Put all the ingredients in a food processor and blend until smooth.

• If a sweeter taste is preferred, add 1 teaspoon soft brown sugar.

CORIANDER AND YOGHURT DIP

MEDIUM-HOT

Thick and creamy, fresh tasting and smooth, this pungent green dip is excellent with fish and grilled chicken, and is just the thing to spike up a plain baked potato.

1 teaspoon cumin seeds, toasted (see page 14)
1 1/2 tablespoons water
5 tablespoons fresh coriander, chopped
Juice of 1/2 lemon
1 teaspoon salt

250 g (9 oz) plain Greek yoghurt
2 fresh green chillies, deseeded and finely chopped
Freshly ground black pepper

Put the cumin seeds in a blender and grind for 1 minute. Add the water, coriander and lemon juice and blend again (scrape the mixture down the side of the bowl if it sticks) until a smooth paste is formed.

Mix the remaining ingredients in a bowl, stir in the paste and blend thoroughly.

• Will keep in the refrigerator for 2 days.

SESAME AND GINGER DIP MEDIUM

This ambrosial combination not only smells good but tastes wonderful too. Serve with spring rolls, deep-fried prawns or wonton.

1 tablespoon cashew nuts, toasted (see page 14)
2 cloves garlic, peeled and crushed
1 tablespoon caster sugar
6 cm (2 1/2 inch) piece fresh root ginger, peeled and finely chopped
1 tablespoon soy sauce

1 tablespoon sesame oil
1 tablespoon tomato paste
1 tablespoon rice wine vinegar
1 teaspoon chilli oil
1 teaspoon dry mustard
1 1/2 tablespoons sesame seeds, toasted (see page 14)

Put the nuts, garlic, sugar and ginger in the food processor and blend until smooth. Transfer the mixture to a bowl and add the soy sauce, sesame oil, tomato paste, vinegar, chilli oil and mustard. Mix together well. Stir in the sesame seeds just before serving.

GUACAMOLE MEDIUM

This all-time favourite from Mexico can be served as a dish on its own, with tortilla chips or nachos.

1 onion, finely chopped
1 stick celery, chopped
2 tomatoes, deseeded and chopped
3 fresh medium-hot green chillies, finely chopped, or 2 dried pasado chillies, soaked (see page 11) and finely chopped
1 1/2 tablespoons fresh coriander, chopped

1/2 teaspoon salt
1/2-1 teaspoon cayenne
1 tablespoon lime juice
Freshly ground black pepper
Flesh of 2 ripe avocados, prepared at the last minute

Put all the ingredients, except the avocado flesh, in a food processor and blend for 30 seconds or until roughly chopped but not mushy. Transfer the mixture to a bowl.

In a separate bowl roughly mash the avocado flesh, then add to the chilli mixture and season to taste.

• Cover with cling film and keep in the refrigerator.

• If you make this dip in advance, the surface may discolour. If it does, scrape off the affected layer – it will not alter the taste.

Right: *Sesame and Ginger Dip*

ROAST AUBERGINE DIP SPICY

This lovely, creamy dip has a delicate flavour which complements skewered lamb, grilled queen scallops, or celery sticks beautifully. Alternatively, serve over grilled goat's cheese.

Preheat the oven to 250°C/475°F/Gas 9.

3 medium-sized aubergines	Grated rind and juice of 1 lemon
1 tablespoon sunflower oil	2 tablespoons fresh mint, chopped
2-3 cloves garlic, peeled and finely chopped	2 tablespoons fresh coriander, chopped
1 fresh medium-hot green chilli, deseeded	4 tablespoons plain Greek yoghurt
and finely chopped, or 1 dried chipotle chilli,	Salt and freshly ground black pepper
soaked (see page 11) and finely chopped	

Put the aubergines on a small baking tray and cook in the oven for 1 hour or until soft. Remove from the oven, split the aubergines down the centre, remove the seed bags and discard. Scoop the remaining flesh out of the skins and set aside. Discard the skins.

Heat the oil in a heavy-based pan over a moderate heat and cook the garlic and chilli for 1-2 minutes. Tip the cooked ingredients, including the oil, into a food processor and add the lemon rind and juice. Blend to a paste. Add the aubergine flesh, mint, coriander and yoghurt and blend until smooth.

Season to taste.

PEANUT DIP MEDIUM

The perfect accompaniment for satay chicken, beef and lamb.

2 tablespoons sesame oil	225 g (8 oz) crunchy peanut butter
2 cloves garlic, peeled and finely chopped	200 g (7 oz) canned coconut milk
2 fresh medium-hot green chillies, finely	1 tablespoon fresh coriander, chopped
chopped, or 5 dried tepin chillies, crushed	Juice of 2 limes
2 sticks lemon grass, topped, tailed,	Sea salt and freshly ground black pepper
and outer leaves removed, finely chopped	

Heat the oil in a heavy-based pan and gently sauté the garlic, chillies and lemon grass for 1 minute.

Remove the pan from the heat and add the peanut butter and coconut milk. Simmer over a low heat for 4-5 minutes, then stir in the remaining ingredients and season to taste.

• Allow the sauce to stand for at least 2 hours before serving.

FRESH HERB DIP MILD AND AROMATIC

As its name suggests, this tasty dip has a fresh, rather spicy taste. Excellent with hard-boiled quail's eggs, raw vegetables or prawns.

1 teaspoon cumin seeds	3 tablespoons fresh parsley, chopped
1 teaspoon fennel seeds	2 cloves garlic, peeled and crushed
1/2 teaspoon black mustard seeds	2 tablespoons extra virgin olive oil
3 tablespoons fresh basil, chopped	300 ml (10 fl oz) plain Greek yoghurt
3 tablespoons fresh chives, chopped	Salt and freshly ground black pepper

Toast the cumin seeds, fennel seeds and mustard seeds (see page 14).

Put all the ingredients in a food processor and blend until smooth.

Season to taste.

CURRIED PINEAPPLE DIP MEDIUM

This colourful dip is bound to impress! Serve with raw vegetables, chicken on sticks, pitta bread or dipping crackers.

1/2 small pineapple, peeled,	150 ml (5 fl oz) crème fraîche
cored and chopped	1 stick celery, finely chopped
4 tablespoons plain Greek yoghurt	1 fresh medium-hot green chilli, finely
1 teaspoon medium curry powder	chopped, or 1/2 dried habañero chilli,
1/2 teaspoon turmeric	soaked (see page 11) and finely chopped

Put the pineapple in a sieve or colander. Using your fists, squeeze it against the sides to extract the juice – this will prevent the dip from curdling or becoming too runny. Discard the juice and chop the pineapple into very small pieces.

Place all the ingredients in a bowl and mix together well.

AILLADE HOT

A wonderful hot, crunchy, garlicky dip. Serve with raw vegetables, grilled prawns or cold meats.

2-3 large cloves garlic, peeled and	2 tablespoons fresh parsley, chopped
finely chopped	2 teaspoons white wine vinegar
1 1/2 tablespoons walnut pieces,	4 tablespoons walnut oil
finely chopped	1 egg yolk
1/2 teaspoon salt	

Put the garlic, walnuts, salt, parsley and vinegar in a bowl and mix together well. Slowly add the oil, 1 tablespoon at a time, stirring continuously.

Add the egg yolk and beat vigorously for a few seconds to emulsify.

• Try pine nuts instead of walnut pieces.

• For extra zing add 1 tablespoon chopped fresh chives.

• This will keep in the refrigerator for 4 days.

SALSAS

'Salsa' is the Mexican word for sauce. Salsas can be fiery hot, traditional, mild or exotic and are made from a combination of contrasting flavours and textures. They are best prepared at least 4-6 hours in advance and left at room temperature, to accentuate the flavours of the ingredients.

All recipes are for four people.

SALSA FROM HELL VERY HOT

This salsa will blow your mind! Serve with grilled steak, tortilla chips, pork and lamb.

• Make at least 4 hours in advance, and keep at room temperature.

1 onion, finely chopped
1 stick celery, chopped
5 ripe tomatoes, deseeded and chopped
2-3 fresh habañero chillies, finely chopped,
or 2-3 dried habañero chillies, soaked
(see page 11) and finely chopped

1 1/2 tablespoons fresh coriander, chopped
1/4-1/2 teaspoon salt
1/2 teaspoon cayenne
1 tablespoon lime juice
Freshly ground black pepper

Put all the ingredients in a food processor and briefly blend until finely chopped but not mushy.

MANGO AND CUCUMBER SALSA HOT

This sweet and spicy salsa has a fiery kick! Wonderful with crab, grilled swordfish or barbecued chicken.

• Make the salsa at least 4-6 hours in advance, and keep at room temperature.

1 large ripe mango, peeled, stoned
and finely chopped
1 tablespoon yellow pepper,
finely chopped
1 tablespoon red pepper, finely chopped
Juice of 1 lime

1/2-1 fresh red scotch bonnet chilli,
deseeded and finely chopped, or 1 dried
habañero chilli, soaked (see page 11)
and finely chopped
1 tablespoon fresh coriander, chopped
1 tablespoon cucumber, peeled and chopped

Put all the ingredients in a bowl and mix together well.

Left: Tomato and Mint Salsa

GREEN SALSA VERY HOT

This is a good all-purpose salsa, excellent with grilled swordfish, kebabs, chargrilled prawns and tortillas.

• Make the sauce at least 4-6 hours in advance, and keep at room temperature.

7 green tomatoes, skinned (see page 14), deseeded and chopped, or tomatillos, husks removed, deseeded and chopped
3 fresh very hot green chillies, finely chopped, or 1 dried habañero chilli, soaked (see page 11) and finely chopped
50 g (2 oz) fresh coriander, chopped

6 spring onions, finely chopped
Juice of 3 limes
2 cloves garlic, crushed
2 tablespoons extra virgin olive oil
1 tablespoon medium sherry
Salt and freshly ground black pepper

Put all the ingredients in a bowl and mix together well. Season to taste.

ROAST PEPPER AND RED ONION SALSA MEDIUM-HOT

This versatile salsa is good with tortilla chips or grilled bruschetta, or toss with hot pasta.

3 red peppers, skinned (see page 14) and chopped
3 green peppers, skinned (see page 14) and chopped
3 yellow peppers, skinned (see page 14) and chopped

1 small red onion, finely chopped
3 tablespoons extra virgin olive oil
2 tablespoons red wine vinegar
5 tablespoons fresh coriander, chopped
2 teaspoons West Indian hot pepper sauce
Salt and freshly ground black pepper

Put all the ingredients in a bowl and mix together well. Season to taste.

TOMATO AND MINT SALSA MEDIUM

This is an outrageously moreish salsa, with a wonderful smoky flavour. Try it with barbecued steak, oysters, tortilla chips, chilli con carne, nachos, tacos, beans and vegetable dishes.

• This salsa is best made 24 hours in advance.

Preheat the oven to 180°C/350°F/Gas 4.

6 ripe plum tomatoes
2 cloves garlic, crushed
1 teaspoon soft brown sugar
1 1/2 tablespoons tomato purée
1/2 teaspoon balsamic vinegar
2 tablespoons walnut pieces, lightly toasted (see page 14)
Juice of 1 lime

2 fresh medium-hot green chillies, deseeded and finely chopped, or 2 dried guajillo chillies, soaked, puréed and sieved (see page 11)
3 tablespoons fresh mint, roughly chopped
1 tablespoon fresh rosemary, chopped
Grated rind of 1/2 lemon
1/2 teaspoon dried chilli flakes
3 tablespoons virgin olive oil
Salt and freshly ground black pepper

Place the tomatoes on a baking tray and roast in the oven until their skins are black. Remove, and put the tomatoes (skins included) in the food processor with the garlic, sugar, tomato purée and balsamic vinegar. Blend for 1 minute.

Transfer the mixture to a bowl and add the remaining ingredients. Season with salt and pepper. Mix together well, then leave to stand at room temperature (not in the fridge) overnight.

RED SALSA MEDIUM-HOT

This is a classic salsa, robust, gutsy and excellent with Mexican food such as enchiladas, tortillas and fresh tortilla chips.

• Allow the salsa to stand at room temperature for several hours before serving, to enhance the flavours.

1 onion, chopped
1 stick celery, chopped
5 tomatoes, deseeded and chopped
4 fresh medium-hot red chillies, finely chopped, or 4 dried ancho chillies, soaked, puréed and sieved (see page 11)

1 1/2 tablespoons fresh coriander, chopped
1/4-1/2 teaspoon salt
1/4-1/2 teaspoon cayenne
1 tablespoon lime juice
Freshly ground black pepper

Put all the ingredients in a food processor and briefly blend until finely chopped but not mushy.

Season to taste.

• For a hotter sauce add a little more finely chopped chilli.

Right: Mango and Cucumber Salsa

SALSA PESTO HOT

This salsa will enhance a wide variety of dishes and ingredients. Try it with chargrilled fish or chicken, goat's cheese or tortilla chips, or tossed with hot pasta.

• Make the salsa at least 4-6 hours in advance, and keep at room temperature.

2 fresh hot green chillies, or 1 dried pasado chilli, soaked (see page 11)
100 g (4 oz) pine kernels
65 g (2 1/2 oz) fresh coriander, chopped

3 tablespoons extra virgin olive oil
4 cloves garlic, peeled and crushed
Juice of 1 lime
Salt and freshly ground black pepper

Put all the ingredients in the food processor and blend for 30 seconds or until roughly chopped.

MELON SALSA HOT

A delicious combination of hot and cool ingredients, perfect with grilled and roast meats.

• Make the salsa at least 4-6 hours in advance, and keep at room temperature.

1 canteloupe melon, skinned, deseeded and chopped
2 fresh hot green chillies, finely chopped, or 5-6 dried tepin chillies, crushed
1 yellow pepper, chopped

1 teaspoon extra virgin olive oil
1 teaspoon rice wine vinegar
Juice of 1 lime
Salt and freshly ground black pepper

Put all the ingredients in the food processor and briefly blend until finely chopped but not mushy.

Season to taste.

BLACK BEAN SALSA HOT

This strong salsa can be served as a dish on its own. Alternatively, try it with red snapper, grilled lobster, swordfish and tuna.

• Make the salsa at least 4-6 hours in advance, and keep at room temperature.

225 g (8 oz) black beans, soaked in water overnight, then drained and cooked until soft but not mushy, or 400 g (14 oz) canned black beans, drained
2 tablespoons extra virgin olive oil
1 red pepper, chopped
1 yellow pepper, chopped
2 cloves garlic, peeled and chopped
Juice of 1 lime

2 tablespoons fresh coriander, chopped
2 rashers smoked bacon, rind removed, cooked until crispy and chopped
1 fresh hot red chilli, finely chopped, or 2 dried chipotle chillies, soaked (see page 11) and finely chopped
1 dessertspoon West Indian hot pepper sauce
Sea salt and freshly ground black pepper

Put all the ingredients in a bowl and mix together well. Season to taste.

BASIC SALSA HOT

Use this classic salsa recipe as the base and add 350 g (12 oz) of your chosen main ingredient. Experiment with tomatoes, tomatillos, papaya, banana, avocados, melon or cucumber.

• Make the salsa at least 4-6 hours in advance, and keep at room temperature. Can be left overnight.

1 onion, finely chopped
1 stick celery, chopped
2 tomatoes, deseeded and chopped
3 fresh hot green chillies, finely chopped, or 3 dried guajillo chillies, soaked, puréed and sieved (see page 11), and 1 dried chipotle chilli, soaked (see page 11) and finely chopped

1 1/2 tablespoons fresh coriander, chopped
1/4-1/2 teaspoon salt
1/4 teaspoon cayenne – more if desired
1 tablespoon lime juice
Freshly ground black pepper

Put all the ingredients in a food processor and briefly blend until finely chopped but not mushy.

Left: Melon Salsa

53

MARINADES AND PASTES

Marinades and pastes (which are thicker than marinades) are seasoned liquids in which meats, fish and vegetables are soaked so that they absorb the flavours and, in the case of tougher meats, are tenderised. Most marinades include an acid (the tenderiser) such as lemon juice, vinegar or wine as well as a selection of herbs and spices. Make marinades in a glass, plastic, ceramic, or stainless steel container, not aluminium.

All recipes are for four people.

SPICED PASTE VERY HOT

Spread this fiery paste over steaks or white fish such as skate or sea bass.

2 fresh bird's eye chillies, or 2 dried ancho chillies, soaked (see page 11) and puréed
2 fresh mild red chillies, or 3 dried New Mexico red chillies, soaked, puréed and sieved

2 shallots, peeled
4 cloves garlic, peeled
2 tablespoons tomato paste
Juice of 1 lime

Put all the ingredients in a food processor and blend until smooth.

• Marinate ingredients for at least 4 hours, turning occasionally.

ORIENTAL MARINADE SPICY

The distinct flavours of ginger, black treacle and honey make this a perfect marinade for barbecued foods. Try it with chicken, fish, seafood or fillet of beef.

1 tablespoon black treacle
2 tablespoons liquid honey
300 ml (10 fl oz) boiling water
300 ml (10 fl oz) shaosing wine or dry sherry

¹/2 teaspoon salt
2 teaspoons finely chopped fresh root ginger
2 tablespoons soft brown sugar

Put all the ingredients in a bowl and mix together well.

• Marinate ingredients for a least 4-6 hours, turning occasionally.

TANDOORI PASTE SPICY

This aromatic paste is made with more than a dozen spices, which accounts for the exotic flavour it gives chicken, lamb cutlets or skewered quail.

2 onions, quartered	2 teaspoons ground nutmeg
5 cloves garlic, peeled	2 teaspoons ground cloves
5 cm (2 inch) piece fresh root ginger, peeled	2 teaspoons ground cinnamon
Juice of 1 lemon	2 teaspoons cayenne
2 teaspoons ground coriander	4 tablespoons groundnut oil
2 teaspoons ground cumin	4 tablespoons sunflower oil
2 teaspoons turmeric	1/4 teaspoon salt
2 teaspoons garam masala	1/4 teaspoon pepper
2 teaspoons ground mace	300 ml (10 fl oz) plain yoghurt

Put all the ingredients, except the yoghurt, in a food processor and blend until a smooth paste is formed. Add the yoghurt and blend until well mixed.

• Spread thickly over the ingredients and marinate overnight, turning occasionally.

• Greek yoghurt will make the texture creamier and richer.

LEMON AND CHILLI MARINADE HOT

This dry marinade really spikes up the flavour of fried fish. Experiment with whitebait, sardines, goujons of sole or herring roes.

1 teaspoon ground white pepper	2 fresh hot green chillies, chopped, or 2 dried
Grated rind of 1 lemon	habañero chillies, destalked and crushed
	2 tablespoons cornflour

Put all the ingredients in a bowl and mix together well.

• For a starter, coat 450 g (1 lb) whitebait – 900 g (2 lb) for a main course – in 1 egg white (2 if a main course), then toss in the dry mixture and deep fry. Serve immediately.

• Try the deep-fried whitebait with a spicy sauce, such as Green Chutney (see page 33) or Spiced Cucumber (see page 34).

SOUTH EAST ASIAN MARINADE HOT

Hot and spicy, this delicious marinade will enhance the delicate flavours of satay chicken or skewered lamb.

4 cloves garlic, peeled	1 teaspoon curry powder
1 teaspoon freshly ground black pepper	2 small fresh hot red chillies, or
2 teaspoons caster sugar	5 dried bird's eye chillies, crushed
2 teaspoons turmeric	4 tablespoons groundnut or sunflower oil
2 tablespoons fresh coriander, chopped	

Put all the ingredients in a food processor and blend until a smooth paste is formed. Add a little more oil if the mixture is too thick.

• Marinate ingredients overnight, turning occasionally.

MARINADE FOR SPARE RIBS

SWEET AND SOUR

Everybody loves the sweet, gooey consistency of marinated spare ribs. Barbecue or chargrill to enhance the flavour.

3 tablespoons honey	3 tablespoons soft brown sugar
3 tablespoons light soy sauce	2 tablespoons tomato ketchup
3 tablespoons shaosing wine or dry sherry	6 cloves garlic, peeled and finely chopped

Put all the ingredients in a bowl and mix together well.

• Paint the ribs with marinade and leave in the fridge overnight, turn occasionally.

MARINADE FOR SEVICHE MEDIUM

The acid in the lime juice 'cooks' raw fish so that the flesh becomes firmer and turns opaque. Use a really fresh fish such as red snapper, sole, scallops, salmon or tuna for best results.

150 ml (5 fl oz) fresh lime juice	1 teaspoon freshly ground black pepper
4 spring onions, cut into thin,	2 tablespoons fresh coriander,
2.5 cm (1 inch) strips	finely chopped
1 fresh medium-hot green chilli,	4 tablespoons sunflower oil
finely chopped	

Put all the ingredients in a bowl and mix together well.

• Make small cuts into the fish with the tip of a knife to allow the marinade to penetrate the flesh.

• Leave fish to marinate for 3-4 hours or overnight, turning occasionally.

Right: Marinade for Seviche

GINGER AND LIME MARINADE SPICY

This versatile marinade is ideal for chicken, beef or vegetables destined for the barbecue.

4 cm (1 1/2 inch) piece fresh root ginger, peeled and finely chopped
5 spring onions, white part only, chopped
Grated rind and juice of 2 limes
1 tablespoon five spice powder
1 tablespoon soy sauce
1 tablespoon sunflower oil

Put all the ingredients in a bowl and mix together well.

• Paint ingredients with the marinade and leave for 4-6 hours or overnight, turning once or twice.

YOGHURT MARINADE VERY HOT AND SPICY

This is a hot, full-bodied marinade – just the thing to pep up grilled chicken or lamb.

2 cloves garlic, peeled
2.5 cm (1 inch) piece fresh root ginger, peeled
1 tablespoon ground cumin
1/2 teaspoon ground cardamom
1/2 teaspoon chilli powder
2 teaspoons paprika
150 ml (5 fl oz) plain yoghurt
2 fresh very hot green chillies, deseeded and finely chopped, or 2 dried guajillo chillies, soaked, puréed and sieved (see page 11)

Put the garlic, ginger, cumin, cardamom, chilli powder and paprika in the food processor and chop finely.

Transfer to a bowl, add the yoghurt and chillies, and mix together well.

• Stir the ingredients into the marinade so they are well covered, and leave overnight.

SINGAPORE MARINADE VERY HOT

Take care – this really is hot! Use to marinate fish, meat or any vegetable destined for the barbecue.

3 tablespoons tomato purée
3 fresh very hot red chillies, or 10 dried bird's eye chillies
6 cloves garlic, peeled
1/2 teaspoon soy sauce
1/2 teaspoon salt
2 tablespoons water
3 tablespoons sunflower oil
Juice of 2 lemons

Put all the ingredients in a food processor and blend until smooth. Transfer the mixture to a saucepan, bring to the boil and simmer for 2 minutes.

• Marinate ingredients overnight, turning occasionally.

SPICY THAI MARINADE MEDIUM

High in flavour and low in calories, this aromatic marinade is bursting with flavour. Wonderful with chicken or pork ribs.

2 shallots, finely chopped
2 cloves garlic, peeled and crushed
2 tablespoons soft brown sugar
1 tablespoon groundnut oil
2 tablespoons fresh lemon juice
3 tablespoons rice wine vinegar
1 fresh red Thai chilli, deseeded and finely chopped, or 1-2 dried tepin chillies, crushed
2 tablespoons fresh coriander, chopped
170 ml (6 fl oz) Thai fish sauce

Put all the ingredients in a bowl and leave to stand at room temperature for at least 1 hour. Then strain and discard the solids.

• Pour the liquid over meat or fish and leave to marinate overnight.

• Leftover juices can be used for basting.

RELISHES, ATJARS AND CONFITS

All recipes are for four to six people.

GRAPE CONFIT SPICY

This confit has a delicate flavour. Serve with foie gras, pâté and smoked meats and pork.

25 g (1 oz) butter	225 g (8 oz) seedless grapes
1 onion, sliced	2 tablespoons white wine vinegar or white wine
2 teaspoons yellow mustard seeds	1 tablespoon sugar

Gently melt the butter in a heavy-based pan over a moderate heat and sauté the onion until soft and pale golden.

Add the mustard seeds, grapes, vinegar and sugar and cook for 10 minutes or until the liquid has reduced and thickened to a syrupy consistency.

SPICED APPLE CHUTNEY MEDIUM AND SPICY

There's something very appealing about spiced apple chutney, especially when it is served with baked ham, cheese or cold meats.

2 tablespoons sunflower oil	1 medium-hot fresh green chilli, finely
1 teaspoon cumin seeds	chopped, or 1 dried pasado chilli, soaked
1 onion, sliced	(see page 11) and finely chopped
2 dessert apples, cored and roughly chopped	50 g (2 oz) raisins
	Salt and freshly ground black pepper

Heat the oil in a heavy-based pan over a moderate heat and toast the cumin seeds for 30 seconds, shaking the pan constantly. Add the onion and cook until golden, then add the remaining ingredients and simmer for 15 minutes.

Season and serve

CUCUMBER ATJAR SPICY

This is a simple recipe. Try it with curry or poached salmon.

1 tablespoon fresh coriander, chopped	1/2 cucumber, deseeded and finely
1 tablespoon fresh mint, chopped	chopped (not peeled)
1 shallot, chopped	Juice of 1/2 lime

Put all the ingredients in a bowl and mix together well.

• This atjar makes an excellent cooler for hot currys. Add 150-300 ml (5-10 fl oz) of plain yoghurt, depending on the amount required.

TOASTED COCONUT CHUTNEY MILD

This is a thick, crunchy chutney – the perfect accompaniment for chicken or shellfish curries.

2 tablespoons groundnut oil	4 tablespoons unsweetened desiccated
2 red onions, sliced	coconut, toasted (see page 14)
1 tablespoon soft brown sugar	1/4 teaspoon salt
1 tablespoon red wine vinegar	1/4 teaspoon black pepper
1 mild fresh green chilli, deseeded and finely chopped, or 1 dried choricero chilli, soaked (see page 11) and finely chopped	

Heat the oil in a heavy-based based pan over a moderate heat and sauté the onions for about 20 minutes or until very soft and caramel coloured.

Turn up the heat, add sugar and vinegar, and cook until the vinegar has evaporated.

Add the chilli and coconut and cook for a further 3-4 minutes stirring constantly – the mixture should be fairly dry but stir in a tablespoon of water if it gets too dry. Season to taste.

AUBERGINE RELISH SPICY

This relish has a delicate, subtle flavour. Serve with koftas, chicken and lamb kebabs and grilled butterfly poussin.

4 tablespoons olive oil	2 tomatoes, deseeded and chopped
2 teaspoons cumin seeds	50 g (2 oz) currants
1 aubergine, chopped	1 1/2 teaspoons salt

Heat the oil in a heavy-based pan over a moderate heat and toast the cumin seeds for 30 seconds, then quickly add the rest of the ingredients and simmer for 20 minutes or until the mixture has a thick consistency, stirring occasionally.

• If the relish needs to be thicker, cook a few minutes more.

CORIANDER CHUTNEY SPICY

Coriander gives this chutney a distinct Eastern flavour. Serve with kebabs, samosas, tandooris and curries.

200 g (8 oz) fresh coriander	1 teaspoon garam masala
2 tomatoes, cut into 8 wedges each	2 cloves garlic, peeled and crushed
2 teaspoon cumin seeds	2 tablespoons lemon juice
1 teaspoon salt	2 tablespoons malt vinegar

Put all the ingredients in a food processor and blend for 30 seconds.

• For mint chutney, substitute fresh mint for the coriander.

TOMATO RELISH MEDIUM-HOT

This exceptional tomato relish is delicious with cold lamb, barbecued fish and grilled tuna.

2 tablespoons olive oil
2 teaspoons yellow mustard seeds
1 onion, sliced
2 cloves garlic, peeled and crushed

2 tomatoes, deseeded and roughly chopped
Salt and freshly ground black pepper
1 tablespoon fresh basil, torn into strips

Heat the oil in a heavy-based pan over a moderate heat and toast the mustard seeds for 30 seconds.

Quickly add the onion and garlic and sauté for 1-2 minutes, taking care not to brown them. Then add the tomatoes and cook for 5 minutes.

Remove from the heat, season and stir in the basil.

HARICOT BEAN ATJAR SPICY

Simple to make, this tasty atjar is excellent with curries, cold meats and chicken.

1 tablespoon olive oil
1 teaspoon yellow mustard seeds
1 teaspoon coriander seeds
1 onion, sliced

400 g (14 oz) canned haricot beans, drained
1 tablespoon vinegar
Salt and freshly ground black pepper

Heat the oil in a heavy-based pan over a moderate heat and fry the mustard and coriander seeds for 2 minutes, shaking the pan constantly.

Quickly add the onion and sauté for 5-6 minutes or until golden.

Add the beans and vinegar and cook until the liquid has almost evaporated.

Remove from the heat and season to taste.

DRIED FRUIT BLATJANG SWEET AND SOUR

An exotic combination of textures and flavours makes this delicious blatjang a rare treat. Serve with pâtés, cold meats, sausages, salamis, cheese or pickled fish.

450 g (1 lb) mixed dried fruits – figs, apricots, dates, apples and sour cherries, for example,
50 g (2 oz) raisins
1 onion, sliced
1-2 fresh medium-hot red chillies, finely chopped or 1-2 dried cascabel chillies, soaked (see page 11) and the flesh scooped out

2 cloves garlic, peeled and crushed
450 ml (15 fl oz) water
300 ml (10 fl oz) malt vinegar
100 g (4 oz) soft brown sugar
1 teaspoon salt

Put all the ingredients in a saucepan and bring to the boil, then turn down the heat and simmer for 30 minutes. Add a little water if the mixture becomes too thick.

Above: *Dried Fruit Blatjang*

HOT YELLOW PEPPER RELISH

HOT AND POWERFUL!

Go easy on scotch bonnets as they are very, very hot!

Try this colourful relish with cold roast beef or cold veal, or toss it with hot pasta.

2 yellow peppers, quartered
1/2-1 fresh scotch bonnet chilli, deseeded
2 tablespoons olive oil

1 tablespoon fresh coriander, chopped
Salt and freshly ground black pepper

Put the yellow peppers under a hot grill, skin side up, and cook until the skins turn black. Remove from the grill, cool and skin. (Alternatively, leave the skins on; they have a lovely 'charred' taste.)

Then place the chilli under the grill and cook until its skin turns black. Remove, but leave the skin on.

Put all the ingredients in a food processor and briefly blend until very finely chopped.

ACKNOWLEDGEMENTS

I have had the good fortune to work with a team whose energy, enthusiasm and sense of humour have proved second to none. I would like to thank all of them for playing their parts with such expertise and exuberance.

In particular, I am indebted to Rose Prince, whose culinary skills have been invaluable. She gave her time so generously and was such a pleasure to work with that I inevitably look forward to other projects. Thanks also to Jose Luke, who, along with Rose, tried and tested virtually all the recipes and made them look so tempting for the photographs.

To my assistant Christopher Leach, who has rushed around, almost demonically, for weeks, fetching and carrying anything from tables to teacups. His contribution has been zestful yet always practical.

I would also like to thank my friend Simon Wheeler for his outstandingly beautiful photographs – they make the book.

Last but not least my sincere thanks to the following companies for loaning and supplying food and props for photography:

Dried chillies:
Dodie Miller
Cool Chile Co.
P.O. Box 5702
London W10 6WE
Telephone: 0973 311 714
Dodie Miller is an expert on the subject and stocks a wide range of Mexican and Spanish chillies.

Specialist Thai foods:
Tawana Oriental Supermarket
18-20 Chepstow Road
London W2
Telephone: 0171 221 6316

Specialist Chinese ingredients:
Peking Supermarket
59-61 Westbourne Grove
London W2 4UA
Telephone: 0171 243 3006

China, tableware and linen:
Designers Guild
277 King's Road
London SW3 5EN
Telephone: 0171 351 5775

Ceramica Blue
10 Blenheim Crescent
London W11 1NN
Telephone: 0171 727 7041

William Yeoward
336 King's Road
London SW3 5UR
Telephone: 0171 351 5454

Summerill & Bishop
100 Portland Road
London W11 4LN
Telephone: 0171 221 4566

Robert Budwig
Telephone: 0181 969 0539

Madelaine Adams
Cobweb Cottage
Stourton Hill
Nr Shipston-on-Stour
Warwickshire CV36 5HH
Telephone: 0608 684 661

Verandah
15b Blenheim Crescent
London W11 2EE
Telephone: 0171 792 9289

Antiques:
Joss Graham Oriental Textiles
10 Eccleston Street
London SW1W 9LT
Telephone: 0171 730 4370

William Sheppee Ltd
1a Church Avenue
London SW14 8NW
Telephone: 0181 392 2379

Sylvia Napier Antiques
554 King's Road
London SW6 2DZ
Telephone: 0171 371 5881

Tiles:
Mosaik
10 Kensington Square
London W8 5EP
Telephone: 0171 795 6253

Fired Earth
21 Battersea Square
London SW11 3RA
Telephone: 0171 924 2272

RECIPE INDEX

Text © 1995 by Sally Griffiths

Sally Griffiths has asserted her right to be
identified as the Author of this Work

Photographs © 1995 by Simon Wheeler

First published in 1995 by
George Weidenfeld & Nicolson Limited
The Orion Publishing Group
Orion House
5 Upper St Martin's Lane
London WC2H 9EA

British Library Cataloguing-in-Publication Data
A catalogue record for this book is available
from the British Library.

ISBN 0 297 83468 I

Designed by Thumb Design Partnership

040 - 648 - 1